# The Reasons We Speak

# The Reasons
# We Speak

## COGNITION AND DISCOURSE IN
## THE SECOND LANGUAGE CLASSROOM

*Miguel Mantero*

Contemporary Language Education
*Terry A. Osborn, Series Editor*

**Bergin & Garvey**
Westport, Connecticut • London

**Library of Congress Cataloging-in-Publication Data**

Mantero, Miguel, 1967–
    The reasons we speak : cognition and discourse in the second language classroom /
    Miguel Mantero.
        p.   cm.—(Contemporary language education, ISSN 1531–1449)
    Includes bibliographical references and index.
    ISBN 0–89789–905–9 (alk. paper)
    1. Language and languages—Study and teaching.   2. Cognition.   3. Discourse
analysis. I. Title: Cognition and discourse in the second language classroom.   II. Title.
III. Series.
P53.M27   2002
418'.0071—dc21                                  2002018213

British Library Cataloguing in Publication Data is available.

Library of Congress Catalog Card Number: 2002018213
ISBN: 0–89789–905–9
ISSN: 1531–1449

First published in 2002

Bergin & Garvey, 88 Post Road West, Westport, CT 06881
An imprint of Greenwood Publishing Group, Inc.
www.greenwood.com

Printed in the United States of America

The paper used in this book complies with the
Permanent Paper Standard issued by the National
Information Standards Organization (Z39.48–1984).

10  9  8  7  6  5  4  3  2  1

**Copyright Acknowledgment**

Extracts from Karen Johnson, *Understanding Communication in Second Language Classrooms.*
Copyright © 1995 by Cambridge University Press. Reprinted with the permission of Cambridge University Press.

For my wife, Laurel.
Without her, I would be without reason.
In all of the senses of the word.

And for Sara, Marisa, Francisco, Olivia, and Lilly.
They have given us all wonderful reasons to speak.

"It is not the consciousness of men which determines their existence, but on the contrary, it is their social existence which determines their consciousness."

Karl Marx, 1932

# Contents

# *Preface*

The present text was envisioned after a conversation with some friends about the current state of foreign language education in the United States. We first began to argue about how things had not really changed and that only the terminology has been evolving without much influence on general classroom practices. For the most part, I believe that those who were arguing this point were playing the role of the devil's advocate. Understanding that contemporary foreign language education and research in second language acquisition has advanced our understanding of the concepts related to language and language learning. However, this put us on a path to discussing the purpose of research within our field. We came to the conclusion that I believe all of us have made at one point or another, in private or public discussions: It is extremely difficult to develop an idea from theory and place it into practice in our classrooms. Although not earth shattering, this idea became the central theme for the present work.

This book emerged when foreign language education was placed into the same field that included literary theory, reader-response research, and discourse analysis—all with the hope of providing a look into how we as teachers interact and react in the classroom and how we can better understand our decisions and those of our students.

What follows is a brief explanation of each chapter and its main purpose. These explanations, although superficial, will give the reader a general guide to the ensuing chapters.

Chapter One, "Bringing Together Cognition and Second Language Acquisition," sets the groundwork for including the notion of cognition and the mind in the field of second language acquisition (SLA). Sociocultural theory is introduced as the mitigating link between the contemporary foreign language classroom (FLC) and the cognitive skills that we, and our students, have and can develop.

Careful attention has been given to defining the terms and concepts "in the negative." In other words, at times it is necessary and clearer to say what something is not than what it actually is.

Chapter Two, "Inside Out," frames the classrooms where we work and defines them in terms of relationships with other historical or educational entities. This chapter also introduces ideas that surround reader response and brings us closer to understanding the role of cognition, discourse, and literature in a FLC. Chapter Two also serves to incorporate the concept of literature and reader response into our ideas that surround SLA.

Chapter Three, "Above All Underlying Discourse," explains and clarifies why this text focuses on cognition and opportunities to engage in dialogue and discourse. Also, some of the prevailing discourse hypotheses are offered in order to show that they all have one element in common. And that by focusing on that element, our language classrooms can be restructured to allow for cognitive skill building, language learning, and, in this particular case, the development of oral proficiency.

Chapter Four, "Affording Opportunities," is rather theoretical and is essential to understanding the claims that will be made later in the text. Here, the text is investigated in the foreign language environment and how the classroom talk that surrounds these texts may be further explained and defined. Central to this chapter is the notion of scaffolding that has become the buzzword of the moment within our circles. What is argued is that "scaffolding," as many of us understand it, is actually being warped when we put, or attempt to put, it into practice. I expect that this chapter will cause most of us to reflect on our own concepts of scaffolding. This chapter provides the rational for focusing on opportunities to enter into discourse through texts and authentic readings.

Chapter Five, "Control of Language and Ideas," presents us with the framework that will allow for a clearer investigation into classroom talk. Both sides of classroom talk—the instructor and the students—are investigated and commented on. What is established here is not just a list of patterns of classroom talk, but an understanding of just how these patterns emerge and may be set into place, knowingly or not, by the instructor and students.

Chapter Six, "Affect and Literary Response," delves into an aspect of teaching foreign languages that has been paid little attention to in SLA theory, that of literary theory. In an initial attempt at offering a SLA literary theory, two well-established literary theories—Text and Defamiliarization Theories—are outlined and then combined to create the pillar of a new, more applicable theory for the contemporary FLC: Three-Fields Theory. Also, a case is made for the use of literature in FLCs. Through this, by defining the purpose the process, in part, for doing so is presented.

Chapter Seven, "Cognitive Construction," places our minds and those of our students within particular settings that benefit the process of developing discourse and cognition in a FLC. In this chapter, readers will be asked to envision their own classrooms and to see how or if they allow cognition to enter into the teaching environment.

Chapter Eight, "Analyzing Cognition and Discourse," places the theory into practice. This chapter introduces the research that was done within the framework outlined in the previous chapters. A brief summary of an initial pilot study is provided as well as the method of transcription used in the data analysis.

Chapter Nine, "The Reasons They Speak," offers examples from a literature-based FLC that demonstrate the various levels of text-centered talk as well as the general outline of classroom activity observed in the same classroom. Of particular importance are the issues that are brought to the forefront when I look closer at student-initiated talk. Within this chapter, the place of readings is further defined according to their role producing meaning for the classroom talk and interaction.

Chapter Ten, "Extending Our Rationale," takes the findings of the previous chapter and further extends their implications for classroom teaching, research, and evaluation. Within this chapter, the text as a tool in the FLC and what that implies for the instructor is further explained.

Chapter Eleven, "Discourse Analysis for Classroom Teachers," outlines a general methodology for classroom teachers who wish to know more about their own patterns of talk in their classrooms. This methodology is specifically designed for teachers who are in the classroom most of the academic day and would like further insight into their own teaching style and classroom interaction.

Chapter Twelve, "Grammar in Discourse," rose from a practical concern. In the contemporary FLC, grammar instruction will always be a concern; such is our reality. What is being offered are suggestions on how to incorporate the current frame of this text with grammar instruction, or rather, correction. A different view of grammar instruction is needed if we are to put into place the inner workings of what is being proposed by this text, and this chapter lays out the first paths for such a view.

Chapter Thirteen, "Discourse and Communicative Competence," takes the concept of communicative competence and relates it to the findings of this investigation. This chapter is particularly useful as an overview for classroom teachers and it will help them relate the sociocultural foundations explained earlier to their own classroom settings.

Although this book is meant to be read from chapter to chapter, it would be possible to treat the beginning chapters as separate elements. However, the reader should note that a complete understanding of the topics introduced and discussed cannot be fully realized without carefully reading the last few chapters where we see examples of the framework provided in action. However, Chapters Twelve and Thirteen are written with the classroom teacher in mind. In these chapters, teachers can read about how to conduct surface-level discourse analysis and how the various constructs shape the notion of communicative competence within their walls.

# *Acknowledgments*

Many people have been instrumental in assisting me with the writing of this book. Although I can only mention a few, I would like everyone who has ever sat still and listened to me or read a few words to know how grateful I am for their input and suggestions. I would especially like to thank the following people: Frederick Jenks, Frank B. Brooks, Elizabeth Platt, and Brenda Cappuccio. Their encouragement and expectations made the challenge an enlightening one for everyone involved. Also, thanks to Teresa Lucas, who, for the price of a couple of cups of coffee, assisted me with the data analysis.

I would also like to thank my family for allowing me to recreate this book many times over during the discussions that began with their questions. You helped me shape and clarify my own understanding. Gracias.

# *Introduction*

The reasons we speak are not linguistic in nature, but psychological. We do not speak based solely on the pure linguistic form of talk or communication. It is the underlying foundation of meaning that affords us the opportunities to speak.

The present text uses this premise to investigate the links between discourse, cognition, and learning a second language (L2). Given that the classroom environment is an artificial, yet, in most cases, productive one, the role of instructor in providing opportunities (i.e., reasons) for discourse is central to further understanding the inner workings of a L2 classroom.

In an era where group work and collaborative exercises have become the approach of choice in language classrooms, we have yet to truly investigate the instructor in an environment that supposedly offers the students the framework to develop oral communication skills and proficiency. In essence, we have placed a magnifying glass over student-to-student interaction and talk, but have yet to bring into focus the teacher in classrooms that are designed around the ideas of building oral proficiency.

Another element of interest in this text comes about by investigating the materials that the teacher uses to try to bring about discourse in the classroom: authentic readings and literature. These materials, one forgets, were not written for the classroom. I doubt that Miguel de Cervantes had in mind a college course when he sat down to write centuries ago. And Octavio Paz wanted his masterpieces to be primarily used for learning a L2? These authors, and countless others, arguably, wanted to affect the readers' mind with their works, and from there the people could and would talk about them, thereby giving their works a new life and individual meaning. How does an instructor incorporate materials like these in order to help the students develop their various proficiencies?

Analyzing classroom talk has helped form and influence current classroom pedagogical practices, curriculum development, and theories of SLA. Most studies on classroom talk that use a sociocultural framework focus on the interaction between students, while viewing the instructor in the peripheral role of establishing the task and monitoring the progress of the students.

Investigating literature-based FLCs to determine if or how instructors assist students in realizing that they also can interpret and use their own experiences in understanding the literature and authentic texts (and becoming "experts" in their own right), and perhaps developing cognitive abilities that may help them develop their language skills, is an important aspect of this text. Moreover, the role of authentic readings and literature and its effects on discourse in a FLC have not been fully understood within a sociocultural framework. Previous scholars have taken a look at "task completion" (i.e., tasks that instructors have designed) by the students and focus on student interaction. But in a FLC that uses literature as the focus for discourse, the instructor rarely provides tasks for the students to perform, only interpretations or reactions to the readings (Kaufman 1996; Knutson 1993; Littlewood 1980; Steiner 1970).

In the following chapters, I will take a closer look at the purpose of literature and authentic material (magazines, newspapers, and so on) in a L2 classroom environment that has been set around the notion of building oral proficiency. Also, the underpinnings of Reader-Response Theory and literary theories are reviewed for the reader. The investigation within this text has also given rise to a "new" theory, defined here for the first time: Three-Fields Theory. Although literary in scope, it is to be applied in L2 classrooms.

Analyzing classroom communication through a new and informative two-prong method that focuses on the opportunities to speak and on the affect of those opportunities (taken or not) on the cognitive level of talk in the classroom as well as the various forms of interaction will be the focus of the data analysis.

Finally, this text concludes with a brief outline of how classroom teachers can analyze their own classroom in terms of patterns of classroom talk and their role in building overall discourse.

# CHAPTER 1

## Bringing Together Cognition and Second Language Acquisition

The study of discourse in a FLC has always been an area that has influenced and divided scholars and students. One may understand classroom discourse to revolve around the instructor where others believe that classroom discourse revolves around issues and ideas, rather than individuals.

Studies that investigate classroom talk (Gass and Varonis 1994; Hall 1995a; Long and Porter 1985; Aljaafreh and Lantolf 1994) have usually focused on elements that affect overall classroom discourse, but that are student-focused studies. Within the foreign language field, the many articles that address the teaching of literature do not deal with the discourse about the text. Students rely on the instructors to assist them in acquiring a L2 as well as cognitive processes that may help them develop their overall proficiency in the L2.

## CLASSROOM TALK

Sustained classroom talk is defined according to Vygotsky's theory (1962), which states that learning through meaningful interactions with one's environment and the people within it are essential to the development of new knowledge. Rosenblatt (1938) further defines Vygotsky's ideas by stating that transaction is an active relationship that the reader and the literary text share in the creation of meaning. Rosenblatt describes this process as a "two-way" transaction that emphasizes Vygotsky's view about learning through meaningful interactions. In Rosenblatt's Transactional Theory, the reader and the literary text share a distinct, reciprocal relationship. Rosenblatt's views fall under Reader-Response Theory and go against the grain of traditional, teacher-guided, text-centered literature activities in FLCs.

The students within this setting often have varied linguistic backgrounds in their chosen L2. They are now presented with an authority, the text, and only one interpreter, the teacher. In most cases, the students have graduated from reading and writing short texts to reading authentic literature and texts, a task that requires a new set of strategies from the teacher and students.

This concept will be essential in providing an understanding of the work that is to follow. Teachers need to keep in mind that sustained classroom talk does not mean just talking. That is, just because there is classroom talk does not mean that it is sustained. When a text is introduced into a FLC, and here the text being referred to is a story, novel, article, or the like, classroom talk will revolve around the particular text, but later I will explain how a transactional view of literature can assist the development of sustained classroom talk.

## ATTITUDES AND GOALS

Davis et al. (1992) studied the attitudes of foreign language students toward literature and found that they were much less positive or virtually nonexistent. Davis et al. concluded that enrollment dropped dramatically from "language-based" courses to "literature-based" courses. The suggestion was made that the teaching styles of the literature-based courses were partly to blame for this dramatic decrease in student participation in upper-level L2 programs.

The reader is reminded that Rosenblatt's goals in the literature-based classroom include the improvement of literacy and communication skills as well as developing an appreciation for literature itself. These goals are ones that evolve throughout the students' experiences with each other, the teacher, and the text.

As instructors, we may believe that we cannot change the attitudes of our students toward a text, literature, or particular readings. They either enjoy the text and the language or they do not. Here, the responsibility is placed on the text and the student and this can be very easy to do and misleading. Students may not be given enough opportunities to enjoy or understand the text because they are knee-deep in trying to understand what the teacher believes important about the text, perhaps because these beliefs will appear on the next exam. Attitudes and opinions are two very different entities. Our opinions as instructors help shape the attitudes of our students. The difficulty arises when we ask for an opinion that has been replaced by an attitude and instructors believe them to be the same.

## DISCOURSE AND LEXICAL LINKING

Often misunderstood for "discourse" in a FLC is the act of defining and lexical linking (Hall 1995a, 1995b), that is, talking about words and using them to drive the classroom talk lexically as opposed to conceptually. Discourse is conceptually based and not lexically based. For example, a student may enter into an exchange on the definition of the word "liberated" with their instructor. The instructor then answers with "freedom." This simple dialogue, based on the utterances of "what is 'liberated' " and "it is 'freedom' " may assist the individual in knowing the definition of the word without entering into a discussion about it, which may include the price of freedom or who really has freedom in the world. In a classroom where the focus is not solely on building vocabulary but on improving conversation and reading skills, lexical linking does little to assist the development of discourse in the FLC according to Hall (1995a, 1995b).

Literature-based FLCs should be focused on the works read and their meaning to the readers (Rosenblatt 1938), and not just on the definitions that assist in their interpretations. However, the research on classroom talk in a literature-based FLC often does not move past an analysis of classroom communication beyond the utterance or dialogue level, which was explained earlier as lexical linking.

## UTTERANCES AND SENTENCES

Before entering completely into the realm of sociocultural thought and discourse, I need to begin by differentiating the basic units of language and linguistics: sentence and utterance. Later, a case will be made for the importance of viewing classroom talk as beginning with the utterance, but it is a distinction between the two that is presented here.

Bakhtin (1986) takes issue with the Saussurean interpretation of langue and parole: the system and the individual act of speaking. Bakhtin critiques the Saussurean concepts because language within this system was mechanical at its core. Utterances exist because there is a linguistic system. Understanding that utterances do have components that may be deemed linguistic, there are other elements of an utterance, more importantly, that are extralinguistic.

Under this rubric then, a sentence becomes part of a language whereas an utterance forms part of the act of communication. We cannot prescribe an ideal length for an utterance, but a sentence has an ideal (grammatical) length. Also, in order for an utterance to be such, it must be spoken to another person in response to something. And also, within the utterance framework, expect a response. We will later underline the importance of the potential for response and its use in a FLC. Furthermore, after reviewing Bakhtin's thoughts, a sentence cannot remain as such if it is framed and used to communicate. Bakhtin goes as far as to suggest that sentences are repeatable, but utterances are not. There has been some discussion about whether or not Volosinov (1973) and Bakhtin are one the same. While not setting out to prove or disprove this claim, if we look at similar lines of thought within Volosinov (1973), he sets out to establish that it is the entity of theme within utterances, the act of communicating in a specific context, that distinguishes them from sentences.

Where we begin to encounter difficulty as language teachers is when we do not realize that sentences and utterances, as understood from this point forward, are different. And that focusing on one or the other will produce a different type of classroom talk. There is a role for sentences in classrooms, and the realities of teaching a foreign language at any level dictate this. But if we ignore the realm of communicating through classroom talk and utterances, then our lessons will stay at the sentence level and this will be reflected in the type of communication apparent in our classroom talk as is shown later.

## SOCIOCULTURAL THOUGHT

Vygotsky (1978) believes that the human mind is, in essence, mediated by the contexts of our daily lives. Mediation, Lantolf (2000) agrees, centers around the notion that humans use language and other symbolic tools to interact indirectly with their environments, and that speech is the primary tool for mediating the human mind.

Vygotsky also makes certain assertions as to speech and thought. He believes, as Lantolf (2000) states, that speaking and thinking are different concepts that, in turn, deserve to be treated differently. Also, further developing the sociocultural view of human learning, Wertsch (1998) underscores the importance of focusing on "tool use" as mentioned by Lantolf. Both Lantolf and Wertsch refine Leontiev's (1981) belief that in order to understand the activity of the human mind in a sociocultural light we must take a closer look at tool-mediated, goal-directed action.

Sociocultural theory also stems from Luria's (1981) belief that the mind is mainly developed as a functional aspect of culturally and socially constructed human behavior. Leontiev adds to Luria's understanding by saying that motivation is an important factor in whether or a not a person appropriates understanding or knowledge. The ideas of Volosinov (1973) carry with them the essence of the purpose of language in a FLC as seen through sociocultural theory production. The tools that are focused on in the FLC are words (language) that assist in mediating the discourse and activity of those involved in using tools while participating in goal-directed action.

Within sociocultural thought, language itself is absent of meaning. It is when language is placed into a social situation that signs and, hence, ideologies are internally created through external experience, which is mediated by and through tools. In a FLC, words can be defined or given their equivalents (casa = house), but this falls short of language-learning goals. Language does not hinge on memorizing vocabulary. Students may also take on the role of interpreters or reinforcers of meaning in the FLC. Meanings and signs in a FLC are socially introduced, reinforced, transformed, or modified through social speech.

## ON THE WAY TO DISCOURSE

It is necessary to identify the two functions of social speech that stem from and turn into dialogue and discourse. Vygotsky (1978) divides social speech into two areas. First, language arises initially as a means of communication between people and their environment. Second, language may be used as a tool to mediate the self as well as one's environment. Understanding that not all speech is designed for communicating with others is central to the notion of viewing discourse in the FLC where more than one language is at play throughout the learning experiences of the instructor and class. Verbal communication between individuals or groups may take the form of utterance, dialogue, or discourse. Each of these has an effect on the classroom talk. In order to fully understand the sociocultural framework, it is necessary to clarify utterance, dialogue, and discourse. The root of communication, be it in a classroom or not, is the utterance. It is important to understand not only the purpose of utterances, but also their limitations in a FLC. Utterances exist within a context that reflects the nearest social situation. Utterances focus attention on communicative goals to be reached through dialogue, but sometimes the understanding of utterances overshadows dialogue in the FLC. As Bakhtin (1986) notes, an utterance is not the completion of language or dialogue, but a continuation.

An utterance's most important function in dialogue, and in the FLC, is one that teachers often forget: an utterance includes within it the possibility of responding to it, therefore creating dialogue and discourse.

Dialogue is but one form of verbal communication. Dialogue, however, can be understood in a broader sense, meaning more than direct verbal communication between two persons. It could be said that all verbal communication or verbal interaction takes place in the form of an exchange of utterances, that is, in the form of a dialogue. Dialogue may include notions from past experiences that one tries to explain to others. Although the dialogues in a FLC do happen viva voce, their historical and social contexts are often ignored or not realized. If one is to experience what another is talking about, then that person must enter into a dialogue with another about past experiences, and as in the FLC, someone's expression of an event will precede another's experience.

With this understanding of utterance and dialogue, discourse is the next category of communication explained by the sociocultural framework. Bereiter's comments encompass the overall meaning and importance of discourse in a FLC: "(FL) Classroom discussions may be thought of as part of the larger ongoing discourse. The fact that classroom discourse is unlikely to come up with ideas that advance the larger discourse in no way disqualifies it. . . . Dialogue, as a part of the FL classroom, is important, but should not be the goal of teachers nor students because we incorporate much more into creating discourse that assists in learning a second language" (1994, 45). Volosinov (1973) presents us with a more philosophical view of discourse of which Wells's concept of progressive discourse is easily identified if not realized: "Discourse (as with all signs generally) is interindividual. Discourse builds on understanding that has come to be over time and various situations with both the students and the teachers acting as speakers and listeners throughout communication" (1999, 68). Discourse extends beyond the dialogic level, which is based on utterances. Discourse is used to clarify ideas, establish concepts, and react and give opinions to others.

As humans communicate through utterances, dialogues, and discourse, we attempt to understand perspectives from the meaning generated through communication. Contexts and schemas in a literature-based FLC are, obviously, brought about or into play by means of language. We must not make the mistake of assuming that by understanding the language we also understand the speaker. It is the "passive understanding" of speech and communication that an instructor has to be aware of in the classroom, because through this understanding classroom and student discourse are affected. This, in turn, may affect how or how much of the foreign language is learned. Part of the foundation of sociocultural thought is based on the processes being mediated by signs and tools that are dependent on the opportunities to enter into dialogue and discourse. This aspect will be further explained and clarified under the heading "intersubjectivity."

## SETTING AND PURPOSE

This text investigates the construction of discourse in a literature-based FLC in Spanish. By a thorough analysis of the classroom talk, the role of the instructor in providing and recognizing opportunities for discourse in the FLC is determined. The purpose of authentic readings in a conversation FLC is clarified and redefined according to the classroom talk observed. Student-initiated talk or opportunities for discourse are investigated in relation to those opportunities recognized or provided by the instructor. Finally, the relationship between cognitive processes and language acquisition in a FLC is clarified through the use of the Florida Taxonomy of Cognitive Behavior (FTCB) and discourse analysis. Also, this text will delve into matters of the role of literary theory, reader response, and the place of grammar in a literature-based FLC. Finally, an introductory and practical guide will be offered for classroom teachers that wish to find out more about the patterns of communication and classroom talk in their own lessons.

# CHAPTER 2

# *Inside Out*

When investigating SLA, it is natural and predictable that the role of the first language (L1) comes into play at one point or another. However, my focus here is not to further explain or rationalize the theoretical constructs of interlanguage (Selinker 1972), but rather to delve into the environment that has assisted in constructing the contemporary literature-based FLC: the literature classroom where the works are introduced, read, and discussed in the L1 (in this case, usually English). By outlining these practices, we can therefore better understand how certain patterns of communication may affect the contemporary FLCs and L2 acquisition.

## DIVERSITY IN BEING

Entering into an investigation about the L2 classroom needs, above all, a clear representation of the various cultures that surround and cross into the ongoing discourse and educational processes. In today's classrooms, more than ever we tend to lean on the surrounding cultures in order to give a much more diverse view of the materials being presented to our students. This "academic leaning" is not necessarily negative. Our inclinations should foster diversity in the classroom. However, at times we lose focus of this diversity and believe it to be one dimensional.

In presenting other cultures—historical, contemporary, or literary—instructors attempt to have students acquire "a diversity in understanding," that is, the ability to understand the various contexts surrounding the material being studied. And this reasoning, arguably, may assist in promoting

**Figure 2.1**
**Framing Classroom Culture**

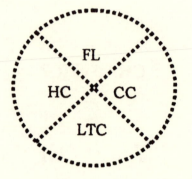

cognitive growth, and in the language classroom, language learning. However, while in the process of understanding humans may change. And it is within this process that the instructor has to realize that even though students may demonstrate a diversity of understanding, each student has acquired "a diversity of being" where new ideas affect his or her outlook on life and, therefore, his or her response to it, cognitively, linguistically, and socially.

## FRAMING CLASSROOM CULTURE

Providing an overall view of the cultural landscape in a language classroom, especially one that relies on literature as its main point of departure, may seem impossible at first, but if we go to our academic foundations, these tasks have already been undertaken.

Figure 2.1 was presented by Frake (1997) after reviewing the methodologies by cognitive anthropologists (Katz and Fodor 1963; Sacks 1972). For the purposes of this text and investigation, this figure has been adapted to take into consideration the L2 classroom.

In Figure 2.1, "FL" represents the FLC that uses literature as its focus for study and discourse (the focus of this text). "LTC" represents the literary culture that the FLC comes into contact with. "HC" is the historical culture that has influenced the FLC and the literary culture. And "CC" is the contemporary culture that influences the FLC and the literary culture. As Frake notes, this framework allows cognitive anthropologists (and other researchers) to view and treat language not as grammatically related, but as conceptually and semantically related. And in doing so, this framework provides us with an early vision of the inner workings of meaning and cognition within individuals and groups.

In reality, culture, in any sense of the word, cannot be so easily divided. It is not the division that concerns us, however, but the idea that our students' responses, while showing that they understand the various influences from the surrounding cultures (many times viewed as the "correct answer" in literature-based FLCs), also demonstrate that their responses are not as easily partitioned because they reflect the surrounding and ongoing influences.

Even the use of the term "culture" when describing the classroom is tenuous. There are those that believe that classrooms cannot be referred to as cultures because of the obvious pitfalls when comparing them to society's cultures. But the term "culture" brings with it the idea structure and knowledge and it is within this that cognition is formed and our minds shared with other members of the particular culture, where our "culture" in the classroom organizes the experiences that we have. Therefore, the opportunities to learn and acquire knowledge or skills are educationally and culturally situated in our classrooms (Goodenough 1971).

## THE WRITTEN WORD

Our memories do not serve us well. This is a human fact. Our minds are limited when we try to recall what was said, by whom, and what we believe was meant by the speaker. That is, if we can remember what they really uttered during our conversation, and this is not to mention what was actually communicated between us. Unfortunately, there is no permanent record of language when it is just spoken. We must make an effort to record the talk (audio or visually) or to take notes if we are to serve our memories well, because they will certainly fail us over time and this will be reflected in the type of dialogue and discourse that surrounds our environments.

Lotman (1988) provides us with a solution to the problem of human memory: writing. Lotman argues that writing (text) serves more to generate meaning than anything else. In this sense, sentences are turned into utterances when they are recalled from a text. This transformation reshapes meaning and the interaction between us, the text, and others. Instructors have often told their students, "Put your thoughts into words." This is difficult enough when you think and write using only one language. When we place a L2 in this equation, our students' writing in the L2 classroom begins to lack for words instead of thoughts. Instructors may equate a lack of vocabulary with a lack of thought in language classrooms and translate that same focus into the texts that they read. The focus is solely on the written word and not the thought behind it, unless it is the teacher's own interpretation. This is then reflected in the exams and other "assessment opportunities" given to students that read a text in a FLC (Bereiter and Scarmandalia 1987), where students repeat the words heard from the teacher without providing thought or mindful interaction.

Writing can be used in the FLC to assist in shaping the thoughts of our students (Murray 1982). Too often, teachers focus on the grammar of the sentence when students write rather than on the thought behind the utterance that gave meaning to the words on the page. All of this happens within certain boundaries and spaces in the L2 classroom, realistically speaking, but these boundaries are to be seen as starting points, rather than limits.

## LINGUISTIC SPACE

There are four basic elements interacting in the creation of linguistic space in a FLC: the instructor, the individual students, the class as a whole, and the texts used in the course. The language of the FLC is not seen as being the only element responsible for creation of linguistic space.

The instructor, of course, has a pivotal role. How we interact with the students and the class, and how we address the text either sets the tone for exploring language and meaning or perhaps just rote memorization and imitation in such as nothing is created, because nothing has changed. Creation, here, is taken as synonymous with change. In the FLC, many teachers believe they are creating language by speaking it and having the students repeat it. But such instructors have forgotten that the essence of language is meaning, and for language to be useful it has to create meaning through discourse.

Leontiev (1981) divides the "account of activity" into three theoretical tiers: activity, action, and operation. Also, mirroring these tiers he develops the concepts of motive, goal, and conditions. So, accordingly, activity and motive are on the first tier, action and goal are on the second tier, and operations and conditions are on the last tier. Furthermore, Leontiev defines "action" as involving a conscious attention to a means-end relationship; "activity" as involving patterns of actions that also provide the context and motive for action; and "operations" as actions and/or activities that have become routinized. In other words, operations are not conscious activities (depending on conditions).

It is within these three tiers that discourse takes place and evolves in the classroom. Wells (1993) applies and redefines Leontiev's three tiers to the contemporary classroom where activity is equated with curricular events and what a teacher plans for each lesson; action is seen as activity related to immediate goals, as such, it is the explanation and practice of a concept; and operation is seen as the actual interaction of events in the classroom that hopefully follow a specific process to become an unconscious activity (i.e., learned).

The main feature of discourse, needless to say, is language, and how language and discourse are defined within the previous framework leads us to Halliday's (1970) idea of systemic linguistics or that all language has meaning potential. Meaning potential takes on various forms at each of the previously discussed tiers. Within the action tier, meaning needs to be negotiated and is not yet agreed on by individuals or the group; in the activity tier, agreed on meaning is used to reach for new meanings; and in the operation tier, meaning has become fully agreed on given certain conditions of the situation and interaction by the individuals and the group.

Halliday summarizes the concept of discourse in one word: register. "Register" is the range of meaning potential in a given situation. Simple enough, but what exactly constitutes a situation? Halliday answers this as well: A situation consists of three different aspects. The first is that of mode where the role of language is defined. The second is that of tenor where the participants' roles are defined. And the third is that of field or the process of what is happening.

Wells (1993) synthesizes these arguments and definitions into a firm concept of what discourse is: We can characterize discourse as the collaborative behavior of two or more participants as they use the meaning potential of a shared language to mediate the establishment and achievement of their goals in social action. In order to be successful in this endeavor, they must negotiate a common interpretation of the situation in terms of field, tenor, and mode and they must make appropriate choices from their linguistic resources in terms of their ideational, interpersonal, and textual metafunctions.

Interestingly enough, the metafunctions listed by Wells correspond to Halliday's field, tenor, and mode. That is, the metaprocesses involved in discourse all have a corresponding mirror image in Halliday's work. As we can see, the initiation, response, and evaluation (IRE) sequence is much less complicated than the view of discourse that has just been reviewed.

The role of the instructor in guiding discourse is extremely important in this framework because it is by his or her interaction with the classroom and individuals that discourse is created, hindered, or neglected. The ramifications of such instructional decisions could be extremely beneficial to students cognitively and linguistically or they could prove to be just reflections of interactions.

A classroom based on the dynamic and developmental communication is not easily realized. Many of these classrooms fall under what Littlewood (1981) and Howatt (1984) call a weak version of the communicative language classroom where interaction and activities are precommunicative. That is to say that these activities are based on more drill and controlled practice than communication, which in turn makes it difficult for discourse as defined earlier to develop within communicative activities. According to Long and Sato (1983), there are certain classroom speech constraints that are due to the conditioned classroom reflexes of the triadic dialogue (i.e., the IRE framework). Nunan (1989, 1987) brings about the idea of using referential questions in order to provide more opportunities for students to engage in communication so as to escape the IRE sequence. These constraints are mainly due to what Nunan (1992) and Kumaravadivelu (1992) term as mismatched teacher intentions and student interpretations. The strategy of using referential questions is as simple as it can be useful if teachers follow Nunan's (1987) outline for what one consists of: asking questions that teachers do not know the answer. According to Long and Crookes (1986), referential questions stimulate learners to engage their "schematic knowledge of representations." As amazingly obvious as this "strategy" may be, many classroom teachers feel uncomfortable asking questions that may not be right or wrong because they place the power in the students' hands and this doesn't fit into the traditional classroom habits (Breen 1985; Van Dijk 1997).

For the purposes of this chapter, discourse and communication are intertwined. In a communicative classroom, as Nunan (1987) notes when he speaks of communication as being supported and explained by negotiation of meaning between the individuals, these individuals then decide whether or not to participate and how they choose to interact or not.

Creating linguistic space in the FLC is not a difficult task if we view interaction as framing the aforementioned triadic dialogue where the instructor is at the center of information giving and getting. But within a linguistic space, interaction must fall within the definition that Kumaravadivelu (1992) links with negotiated interaction: The term "negotiated interaction" denotes the learner's active involvement in clarification, confirmation, comprehension checks, requests, repairing, reacting, and turntaking and in using communication strategies such as circumlocution and paraphrase. Above all, the modifier "negotiated" means the learner should be given the freedom and encouragement to initiate meaningful interaction, rather than simply reacting and responding to teacher talk.

The central idea stated earlier, that of learners initiating meaningful interaction, seems simple enough, but when confronted with the reality of a L2 classroom that is supposedly building communicative competence through the readings and discussions of literature, many classrooms fall short of achieving this goal. Pica and Long (1986) also mention this shortcoming of many L2 classroom environments, but rephrase the concerns in terms of the direction or flow of information. They comment that teachers have been too busy structuring discourse in one direction only, from teachers to student. Pica and Long, in the same study, state that students need to use the information that they have, which is unavailable to the teacher, in order to initiate and enter into negotiated interaction with each other as well as the instructor.

So, after students have entered into "meaningful interaction" is that to be the ultimate goal? Are students and teachers across the land going back and forth, forever trying to convince each other of their interpretation? Hardly. Sooner or later an agreement is reached, an understanding of the other's ideas and opinions that the process of discourse has produced. This "coming to terms" through discourse and negotiated interaction is what Rommetveit (1979b) calls intersubjectivity. Where those involved in communicating must enter into an exchange that extends their own single, private realities that may be very different from their first original interpretation of the event or text.

Intersubjectivity does not have to be class wide. That is to say that every member of the class does not have to agree on the one popular meaning discussed or given, because it would bring us back to the triadic dialogue. Intersubjectivity works on the collective and individual level. It helps each one of us understand, through dialogue, what another person means. Here, understanding of another viewpoint, and not agreement, is the end goal. In the IRE sequence, understanding is often misused for agreement. Students may not understand, but they might agree with the instructor just because they are the ones with the "information."

Coupled with intersubjectivity is alterity. Alterity is a more humanistic, poetic aspect of intersubjectivity, but what is a classroom if it is not human? Bakhtin (1984) expresses alterity in terms of understanding the world through the eyes and views of others. Here, people succeed by becoming a part of the overall whole of society that, in turn, helps to identify the individual as he becomes aware of himself through interaction with others.

When interpreting literature, it is easy to have others tell us what the readings should mean to us. But does this lead to a better understanding of the text (and discourse)? In order to come to an understanding, we have to realize that what builds the text (discourse) around us also affects us.

When we begin to think of what "text" consists of, it is useful to contrast this with "print" as Curtain and Pesola (1994) define further. They make the distinction between two different types of print—environmental and functional—that are useful in a L2 classroom, but may not be as abundant in the literature-based conversational-level classroom. Environmental print is seen as "posters, bulletin boards, displays . . . signs, calendars, and so on" (128). Functional print falls under "the type of information that communicates needed information of immediate value to the reader . . . such as labels, directions on packages . . . , and TV, radio, and cable guides" (128).

We could take a pedagogic leap and place "text" under this heading, but this would be a very constraining definition and would not include an essential part of the process of discourse and interaction in the L2 classroom environment: the learners. For the purposes of this text, Fairclough's (1993) view of what constitutes text is central to understanding the role that discourse has in developing communicative competency: The idea of text, in this framework, brings about the importance that discourse produces text and meaning either in written or spoken forms.

Floriani (1994) notes that if we take into consideration this view of text then we can see how each student can contribute to the interpretation and creation of text not only just with one-on-one student-teacher dialogue, but also with involving the whole class in the creation and interpretation of a text, which then would hopefully facilitate the creation of more opportunities to use the target language and for cognitive growth as well. Also, Floriani points out the cognitive and linguistic skills that individual students have at their disposal are essential when it comes to monitoring their linguistic interaction and their actions. These skills then will aid in interacting with others and recognizing language and patterns of communication, as well as their own.

Viewing text as more than just the printed word enables the students to approach materials in a more dynamic, personal, and interpretive fashion where meaning is to be negotiated through (the creation of) discourse. But for discourse to begin, the opportunity must be given to the students.

One may say that culture and language are inseparable. But in the FLC, unfortunately, language may seem to take precedence over culture. In cultures, and in context, individuals and groups use language to interact and create meaning that in turn creates culture. There has to be some negotiation of meaning between individuals for linguistic space to be created. This linguistic space then interacts within a context or culture.

If we envision a FLC where triadic dialogue is the dominant form of teacher, student, and class interaction, then "culture" is not treated as something to understand only to memorize, such as the holidays, capitals, and famous explorers. But in a FLC where linguistic space is being taught through discourse about culture, some topics of conversation could cover the reason for siestas and the reaction of students that try to understand the cultural meaning of such daily events and if they could ever happen in places like the United Sates. Discourse that is grounded in cultural and personal context/text creates a linguistic space in which students help each other understand, through the L2, each other, their teacher, and various cultures.

Let us not forget the ultimate goal of the FLC: to learn the L2. Creating a classroom that welcomes open-ended questions from the students and teacher alike is not easy, but it can be done at various levels of instruction.

## ISEREAN READERS

Viewing our students as having the potential to be different readers, theoretically at least, assists us in developing approaches in our language classrooms when we implement literature or authentic texts. Iser (1978) begins by offering two relatively all-encompassing categories of readers: real and hypothetical. Within each of these categories, there are subcategories that may assist the instructor in understanding and guiding the responses that students have in their classrooms.

Real readers, as the term states, are those readers that have been studied and their reactions have in some way been recorded, quantified, or noted in one way or another. These are the readers that appear in investigations such as this one, where we may be able to draw some comparisons with their performances and reactions in the classroom.

The next group of readers, hypothetical readers, can be further divided into ideal and contemporary readers. It is crucial that we understand that these are hypothetical constructs that hinge on the effect the reading has on each type of reader.

Ideal readers, according to Iser (1978), almost reflect the author. This ideal reader can understand the author's images, language, and purpose perfectly. For the ideal reader, there is no mystery in interpreting the text. If we look back at the real readers that we have taught in our classes, very few, if any, seem to come close to the "ideal reader." As instructors, we are often thrust into the role of the ideal reader for our classes, but can we really say that we understand every nuance of meaning and context of a particular text as if we wrote it ourselves? What is actually present, hopefully, in the classroom are real readers guiding each other through a text.

The contemporary reader, hypothetical as well, takes the text being read and understands it by reconstructing the history that surrounded the text when it was being written. This history takes into account the daily aspects of the author's life, the social aspects of the place where the author lived, and the general literary and global climate in which the author composed the work being interpreted. We might tend to label our students as contemporary readers if we present them a context- or schema-building lesson about the time in which the author lived and wrote. But it is a big step, linguistically and conceptually, from understanding the contexts and background information to seeing how they affected the author's writing. Students are usually told by the instructors about how these may have influenced the author's viewpoint. And the students take this information without really developing the ability to do so on their own.

The different types of readers, according to Iser (1978), have one element in common. They all rely on the text to produce results. In a manner of speaking, this is obvious, and perhaps oversimplified. But what is not mentioned is worth expressing as well. As instructors, we cannot rely solely on the text to produce results. As will be later explained, the purpose of using literature in the L2 classroom is not to reproduce the text but to produce opportunities to enter into discourse that may affect linguistic proficiency and cognitive skills.

## READER RESPONSE

Attempts at making sense out of literary works require that students take a particular stance (Iser 1978). This stance, as explained further by Liaw (2001), allows the reading to come alive in the student's mind over time. This stance is not static, but dynamic and fluid. Also, the incorporation of a reader-response approach to the teaching of literature may assist in building motivation in the overall classroom setting (Ali 1994; Elliot 1990). The purpose of such an approach is to incorporate the humanistic-aesthetic aspect of education (Skutnabb-Kangas 2000). If students and instructors adopt this perspective when reading literature, then literature is treated as an art form that has been brought into the classroom instead of a lesson plan that originated in guidelines and curricula (Liaw 2001; Rosenblatt 1938).

Within the reading-response framework, Hynds (1992) argues that even in the L1 literature classrooms of English or language arts the teacher may unknowingly affect students' responses. As Hynds states: "Although much literature and reading instruction centers on asking questions about texts, we are not sure if questioning has any more effect than other instructional strategies in getting students to think about what they read. Looking beyond the types of questions that teachers pose, we might begin to explore the questioning practices of teachers and the influence of these practices on student achievement and understanding" (81).

Underlying these statements is the notion that just asking and answering questions in a classroom does not necessarily constitute communication. If we take these claims and transfer them into the FLC, it becomes necessary to add a linguistic level to the patterns of communication. Unfortunately, foreign language teachers may be focusing on the linguistic complexity of their questions and not the cognitive skills or abilities that students may need to understand and respond to the questions in the L2. Chou et al. (1980) comment that during the 1970s a teacher's questions in a literature classroom only moved into the realm of inference relatively few times during the course of a lesson. More than twenty years later, the present investigation, after all of the attention that has been placed on reader response in L1 and L2 classrooms, demonstrates that the pattern of communication has not changed very much, if at all.

## EDUCATIONAL LINGUISTIC BEHAVIOR

Throughout Anderson and Rubano's (1991) research, we see almost a mirror image of the foundation for aesthetic reader response in a L2 classroom when compared to the L1 classroom where literature is being taught: opportunity. An instructor must offer opportunities for students to enter into discourse and aesthetic responses about the text. But there is a major foundational concern in the FLC, and that is language. Instructors and students, according to the educational practices mentioned by Chou et al. (1980) and Cooper (1985), become accustomed to the "linguistic behavior" instead of a literature classroom in the L1. Therefore, the mind or cognition in the L2 classroom often takes a backseat to the "linguistic goals" that were reinforced in the L1 classrooms.

Beach (1993) writes about various developmental phases that students go through when learning how to respond to and read literature in the L1. The students' abilities to interpret and understand the materials develop, hopefully, over time and after exposure to sources in the L1. This psychological theory of reader-response development when placed in the L2 class-room requires us to believe that a student's cognition is independent of the language being taught. Although we believe that they are independent, this does not mean that by approaching one through the other that we cannot assist students in strengthening their linguistic or cognitive skills. Elkind (1981) addresses this as learning how to think and teach in a new key where we have more than one skill or ability being used and developed at the same time.

## ONLY L1 COGNITION?

It is just as important for this linguistic behavior to include students talking about what they are learning, the difficulties, as well as the successes as Beach (1993) points out. But when we try to transfer this thought into the language classroom, students' successes and difficulties are defined in terms of linguistic proficiency instead of cognitive problem-solving abilities. So, if any student-to-student talk occurs during the lesson in a literature-based FLC, as shown in this study, more than likely it will be linguistically directed by the instructor and not oriented toward challenging the thinking processes.

There have been some scholars that have supported an approach to lit-erature that in essence redefines the various roles of students and teachers in a literature classroom (Kramsch 1993; Osborn 1998). This redefining of roles will be even more useful in the L2 classroom where for the most part cognition has unfortunately been attached to those processes that can only be regulated and performed in the L1. Accordingly, if we use our skills as instructors to motivate our students' minds then literature becomes an art form that has been shaped by language (Stone 1990).

In an attempt to present a model of literary understanding, in other words, the elements involved in the cognitive processes of the reader's mind, Purves (1985) presents us with the basic elements of writer, reader, text, and audience. Within this particular framework, meaning is created when the reader has a shared cultural and contextual background with the writer, the text, and the audience. Of great importance in this model is that the writer and the reader differ in the personal significance that the text may have, in turn creating varying interpretations and understandings. The au-dience plays a crucial role because it is a target audience, so this shapes the writer's thinking and writing process. What the language teacher that uses authentic texts or literature in the classroom has to realize is that not even the instructor knows for sure what the writer had in mind (i.e., the personal significance) while he or she was writing. One can study the audience of the time and try to understand what the author had in mind, but this by no means can be an absolute truth. And there lies part of the problem when we take literature into the L2 classroom. Students are for the most part presented with a text that was meant for personal interpretation, but are asked to delve into the mind of an author that has been assigned absolute truths by an audience that was not part of the original framework or thinking of the author. And we wonder why students, at times, do not seem to "understand" literature in our classes? We are placing literature above language in hopes of promoting literacy. But does literacy begin or end with language? As Sapir (1921) and Whorf (1956) mention in their investigations: Language is what holds our communities and our cultures together. As these words and utterances are placed into context, they produce semantic relations with the world in which we live that was harvested by authors to bear fruit in the pages of their texts. But bear in mind that this fruit will not ripen until a cover has been opened and the pages turned. In order for language to be the beginning of literacy and to assist in language learning, the instructor must allow for language to be produced, not reproduced, in the classroom with guidance from the knowledge passed down from generation to generation to the students coupled with the opportunity to implement that knowledge during classroom activities and communication

It should come as no surprise that throughout this text references are made to foundational thinkers and scholars, such as Sapir and Whorf. To try to understand an idea, and to interpret it, it is necessary to go to the source of that idea itself, rather than to someone else's interpretation, however valid it may be.

## OVERVIEW OF APPROACHES TO READER RESPONSE

This section is a summary of most of the possible approaches to reader response in a literature-based classroom. Depending on the framework or theory from which we operate, our classrooms will embody these approaches. This section is not meant to be an all-inclusive analysis of each theory, but it is meant to serve as a guide to those of us who are not as familiar with the field of literary theory or reader response.

Political approach: Our readings have been written within a specific context and historical environment. Every reading is supported, consciously or not, by ideologies. These beliefs, in turn, shape our texts. It would be difficult if not impossible to write a text free of ideology. This approach tends to try to understand what the author wanted to accomplish ideologically from writing the text, or perhaps how the text was shaped by the beliefs surrounding the author at the time. A close reading through this approach places the reader's ideologies along with the author's in which the reader may understand his or her own better after investigating the author's ideological underpinnings.

Processing approach: Here, the reader completes the meaning of the text, but the text has set the ground rules for interpretation. Complete understanding and meaning takes place solely between the reader and the text.

Personal context approach: Although we may understand that a text was written during a specific time period and in a certain context, we approach a text in this manner by attempting to make use of our shared history (or histories). Understanding may take place when the reader appropriates an understanding of the historical surroundings of the text, but the reader may also have different views that may not be shared by the author or the text.

Structuralist approach: The issue of reader competence comes into play during this approach rather than during the others. The reader has to be familiar with the style and type of text; in other words, the type of genre that it encompasses. An effective reader can take advantage of his or her overt knowledge of the text in order to comprehend it. If a reader is to completely understand a poem, then he or she must be familiar with the particular type of poetry in order to bring the meaning out of the text.

Subconscious approach: The reader during this approach is unaware of exactly just how the text is affecting his or her conscious response to it. But what is important is that with a close reading of the text, the subconscious meaning gathered by the reader changes the reader's own reactions and beliefs. This is a very personal response to literature that begins within the students.

Each one of the approaches mentioned will treat language and meaning differently. In a language classroom, each approach has its limitations, but what is important to realize is the approach that we subscribe to as teachers who rely on literature to provide information, linguistic or not, to our students. Of the approaches outlined, it is not necessary to side with only one, but to understand how each approach affects classroom talk that surrounds texts. If our goals and objectives include the improvement or development of oral proficiency in the L2, then a structuralist approach would not allow much room for negotiation of meaning or discourse between students or teachers, as will be shown later.

## OUT OF LITERATURE AND INTO SLA

The understanding that literature-based FLCs have a challenging task ahead of them is an understatement, at the very least. But if nothing else, after interacting with these pages the reader will comprehend how the effective use of literature in a language classroom can promote SLA. Our basic concern as foreign language teachers, stated or implied, is the learning of the L2, and hence the crux of our current issues. Lazar reinforces the reasons why we should approach literature in a L2 classroom from a reader-response or cognitive framework: "Focusing on a task that which demands that students express their own personal responses to these multiple levels of meaning can only serve to accelerate students' acquisition of language. Acquisition may also be accelerated because the overall context for processing new language is so striking" (1993, 17).

And, it is this that we hope to achieve: by approaching our students through cognitive and linguistic resources in order to help them learn a new language and perhaps acquire and improve their cognitive skills. If we enter the language classroom with a "cognitive" frame of mind, then we might be able to provide better opportunities for our students to acquire the L2 through discourse.

# CHAPTER 3

⌒⌒

# *Above All Underlying Discourse*

In selecting an instrument to assist with the analysis of classroom talk, one essential criterion had to be met: the method had to take into account "cognition" in the naturally occurring talk and interaction in the FLC. This proved not to be an easy task, and some may disagree with the final decision, but those that do must keep in mind the framework and purpose of this research and text: to investigate classroom talk through a sociocultural lens that holds true the understanding that our minds, in effect, cognition, have as much to do with learning processes, if not more, than the languages that we speak in order to achieve our goals.

As we shall see, the instruments selected take into account that talk-in-interaction is collaborative in nature (Sacks, Schlegoff, and Jefferson 1974). Also, these collaborations do have an effect on an individual's cognitive processes in SLA (Hymes 1972). While still upholding the sociocultural view of discourse analysis, it is necessary to mention three basic underpinnings of talk-in-interaction described by Heritage:

- Conversation has structure
- Meaning of a particular utterance is shaped by what immediately precedes it and also by what immediately follows it
- There is no a priori justification for believing that any detail of conversation, however minute, is disorderly, accidental, or irrelevant (1988)

Especially important for our purposes and understanding is the second assertion that places meaning in a dynamic state where intention and expectation may fall prey to the linguistic behavior and limitations of students and instructors only to bring about patterns of communication that (as we shall see) do little to assist cognitive growth in the FLC. As instructors, we do provide lesson plans and structure our classrooms a priori. It is essential that we do this. In no way is it being suggested that L2 classrooms become playgrounds of meaning where students are not truly evaluated on their abilities and skills. But the structure of lesson plans are geared toward goals and objectives of a certain class or course, and these goals and objectives should be met, realistically. If we write down that a goal of the course is to improve overall oral proficiency, then we must be responsible for structuring our lessons and classroom activities toward that goal. Also, if we structure classes toward particular goals, then we must be able to evaluate our students appropriately and effectively.

## STRUCTURES AND FUNCTIONS

Discourse analysis has a long and respectable history of focusing on the structures and functions of talk in the language classroom (Grimes 1975; Sinclair and Coulthard 1975; Chaudron 1977; Dressler 1978; Cathcart 1983; Schiffrin 1986, 1987, 1990; Slobin 1991; Learner 1994; Long 1996, 1997; Mackey 1999). Within these frameworks, the following units of analysis that were outlined by Chaudron (1988) are commonplace and serve various purposes:

**Structural**

Utterance—a string of single speech by one speaker under a single intonation

Turn—any speaker's sequence of utterances bounded by another speaker's speech

T-unit—any syntactic main clause and its associated subordinate clauses

Communication unit—any independent grammatical predication; may include elliptical answers in oral language

Fragment—any utterance that does not constitute a complete proposition (i.e., with an explicit subject and verb)

**Functional**

Repetition—repeating of a previous string of speech

Expansion—a partial or full repetition of speech that modifies some portion of a previous string of speech by adding syntactic or semantic information

Clarification—a request for further information from an interlocutor about a previous utterance

Comprehension check—speaker's query as to whether or not he or she has understood the previous speaker's utterance

Confirmation check—the speaker's query as to whether or not the speaker's expressed understanding of the utterance is correct

Repair—an attempt by a speaker to alter or rectify a previous utterance

Model—a type of prompt by a speaker (usually a teacher) intended to elicit an exact imitation or to serve as an exemplary response to an elicitation

Although these units of analysis can be used to give us valuable insight into the L2 classroom, they have two limitations that make them impractical for this investigation, and if used, would not shed any more light on the learning or teaching that happens in a FLC. These limitations are:

1. The foundation of the analysis is the utterance.
2. An understanding of cognition and mind is not built in to this type of functional analysis.

The basic unit of analysis is the utterance. The analysis of classroom under this rubric does not extend beyond what Chaudron has described as the utterance. In order to move beyond the utterance level of communication, the present investigation extends itself into the dialogue, discourse, and progressive discourse levels—all of which appear, at one point or another, in our classrooms. To ignore the extended use of utterances and just focus on one at time would not give us a complete picture of the process of SLA or cognition in our classrooms.

If we review the previous functional units, it is extremely difficult to assume any cognitive values to the utterances being analyzed. These units are, for the most part, part of almost any FLC. What is missing from the functional units is an understanding of the mind and cognition that supports and influences these functions. It is dangerous to assume the underlying cognitive foundations or reasons for any of these units of analysis, so it is necessary and crucial that I introduce the FTCB (Givens 1976), which will be further explained later.

Later on, I will discuss the role of communicative competence in a literature-based FLC. Part of my discussion will include the construct of discourse competence. As part of the revision, suggestions will be made on how to better understand discourse competence within a sociocultural framework.

Markee (2000) suggests the following methodology for approaching analysis of discourse and cognition in the language classroom. The reader should note the importance of understanding the wholeness of communication and of how cognition is constructed. The methodology should be:

- capable of identifying both successful and unsuccessful learning behaviors, at least in the short term.
- capable of exploiting the analytical potential of fine-grained transcripts.
- capable of showing how meaning is constructed as a socially distributed phenomenon, thereby critiquing and recasting cognitive notions of comprehension and learning.

By using a two-pronged approach, this study will demonstrate the process of classroom communication by focusing on the levels of utterance, dialogue, and discourse and by providing an understanding of the cognitive levels of classroom talk and their effects on the whole of communication and perhaps SLA.

## SIMILAR HYPOTHESIS

The analysis of the construction of discourse has led to many different hypotheses, and while it is not the intention or purpose of this book to explain each one, it is imperative to point out the one notion that they all have in common: opportunity.

The Interactional Hypothesis (Long 1981, 1983, 1985a, 1985b) focuses on the importance of comprehensible input and, as Johnson (1995) states, conversational adjustments. These conversational adjustments allow the speakers and learners to take advantage of opportunities to interact and to use the L2, therefore promoting SLA.

Swain's (1985) Output Hypothesis takes the notion of input and makes certain that we understand that it is only one-half (at the most) of the SLA equation. Swain underlines the roll of the opportunities to create output in the L2 in order to assist in the SLA process.

In the Topicalization Hypothesis (Long 1983; Ellis 1984), the focus is on opportunities for students and learners to choose and control the topic of the conversation. This, then, naturally turns into the Collaborative Discourse Hypothesis.

Ellis (1990) brings to light his Collaborative Discourse Hypothesis in which the communicative context as a driving force in SLA takes hold. Ellis also explains that opportunities appear as students and teachers take part in communication and discourse, and this, in turn produces more occasions for SLA.

Now when we take a step back and study the previous hypotheses, the importance of opportunities in learning a L2 becomes overwhelming. And this, in part, is why the discourse analysis presented focuses on opportunities present (or not) to construct meaning and discourse, which in turn affect cognition.

If teachers choose to subscribe to only one particular theory, then they will still have to pay attention to the role of opportunities within that particular theory. Although sociocultural theory is being used as the driving force behind the importance of opportunities in the L2 classroom, one may choose to hold another theory over the current one that is being supported. In this instance, it is not "do or die." A person does not have to embrace the whole of sociocultural thought to understand the importance of opportunities in creating discourse in the L2 classroom. But it is believed that a sociocultural framework is what best complements the role that opportunities play in shaping language and cognition.

Although we could have relied on Bloom's *Taxonomy* (1956), the FTCB, when used with the transcripts, turns out to be a very effective instrument in discourse analysis. Even though some believe the FTCB to be outdated, I say that at the very root of language structure and function is cognition, our minds, and what we mean when we speak. It is only when we value this that we can understand what we do with language and are able to further investigate its structure. We should not place "an expiration date" on ideas because they never really disappear. Foundational ideas may change form or be applied in various contexts, and while doing so some terminology may change; however, the root of these ideas remains as an integral part of current thinking. It is this root that is most important to our current understanding and for the use of the FTCB.

# CHAPTER 4

⬥

# *Affording Opportunities*

Learning a L2 has as much to do with the psychological processes of human development as it does with the formation of the linguistic system. In trying to understand the dynamics of FLCs or L2 classrooms within sociocultural thought, various terms and concepts must be clarified and defined.

Wertsch states that "[t]he basic goal of a sociocultural approach to mind is to create an account of human mental processes that recognizes the essential relationship between these processes and their cultural, historical, and institutional settings" such as classrooms (1991, 6). Given this statement, we cannot help but think of how students, classes, and teachers are affected by their surroundings. If we are to "account [for] human mental processes," it is necessary to explore the elements that affect those processes and what the reactions or outcomes of those processes might be.

## AUTHENTIC TEXT AND LITERATURE IN THE FLC

Incorporating authentic readings into the FLC has been an area of interest from various perspectives: reader response (Elliot 1990; Davis 1989, 1992; Taylor 1985; Frey 1972; Hankins 1972), the value of reading and communicative competence (Hall 1999; Loureda Lamas 1999; Nunan 1987; Spada 1987; Hester 1972; Leal 1999), and learner-centered methodology and teacher roles (Swaffar 1998; Bernhardt 1995; Tudor 1993; Lazar 1990). This research suggests that literature and other authentic readings can be used to address the issues of how communicative strategies may be enhanced by the use of authentic readings. Moreover, that instructors should center the interpretations around more aesthetic responses does not clarify the type of discourse nor the most effective type of interaction in a literature-based FLC. In other words, the effect of literature on the whole of classroom discourse has not been studied thoroughly. These authors suggest uses for literature, but they do not conduct any classroom-based research on its effects on the pattern of discourse in a FLC.

There are also studies that do allude to the notion of literature and authentic readings in a FLC, but it is done as a cultural component of the overall curriculum. Discourse (as understood by this text) is not the focus of such studies (Barnes 2000; Kempf 1995; Davidheiser 1977; Steiner 1972), instead, how students can be presented with culture is their main objective. This type of research offers very little insight into how discourse evolves around, through, or because of literature.

An area of interest is the researching and theorizing about the strategies for teaching literature and other authentic texts in a FLC (Katz 1996; Kaufman 1996; Chamot 1994; Knutson 1993; Akyel and Yalcin 1990; Kumaravadivelu 1992; Harper 1988; Blackbourn 1986; Littlewood 1980; Santoni 1971; Steiner 1970). These writings present important methodological issues and strategies, but they do not attempt to exemplify what happens in the classroom after the instructor has used these strategies. Discourse is seen as a given product when using these strategies. This discourse, which in the previous research is not defined, may or may not be realized because of the lack of research that follows from the pedagogical suggestions. In order to benefit fully from suggestions such as these, a complete analysis of discourse as it revolves around literature in a FLC is needed.

Other investigations that revolve around discourse and the classroom (e.g., Kumaravadivelu 1999, 1993; Floriani 1994; Wells 1993; Devitt 1989; Nunan 1989) focus on the cognitive benefits of providing discourse and opportunities for progressive discourse in classroom settings across subject areas. In these writings, the development of discourse and the development of cognition are intrinsically linked. Although these studies focus on discourse across subject areas, the literature-based FLC is not mentioned. Readers are left to imply the benefits of discourse on cognition and learning. The implications brought to light by these scholars are worth investigating in a literature-based FLC.

Within the studies of the FLC, another area of interest has been that of teacher-focused investigation in relation to authentic readings and literature (Graden 1996; Isenberg 1990; Pica and Long 1986; Moskowitz 1976). In these investigations, the idea of discourse is narrowed to that of teacher talk. This framework, although helpful for teacher-education purposes, does not clarify an understanding of discourse in FLC that this present study will establish. Moreover, these studies center around regular FLCs and not literature-based FLCs that focus on summative rather than formative discourse.

Even the sociopolitical implications of using literature in a FLC have been investigated (Delpit 1998; Pennycook 1998). And even though, as Delpit states, we seem to be teaching the correct form of the "dominant discourse," that discourse is neither defined nor exemplified through actual transcripts. Only the implications of using the dominant language (in the previous cases, standard English) in conjunction with culturally weighted material is investigated.

Finally, some scholars have investigated overall language use, cognition, and social interaction in the classroom (e.g., Deyes 1974; Halliday 1993; Kumaravadivelu 1999, 1993; Lightbown 1990; Walz 1993), but these writings focus on the potential of combining context and opportunity to use one's language. Understandably, the literature-based FLC is not mentioned nor is the concept of discourse (as defined for the presently understood). In order to make use of the findings and conclusions from the earlier writings, it is necessary to investigate further the role of cognition and social interaction in a FLC.

Interestingly, further research in the FLC (e.g., Carter and Long 1990; Bretz and Persin 1987; Peck 1985; Myunskins 1983; Meade 1980) has not focused on the role of the teacher and literature or authentic readings in establishing or providing opportunities for discourse. Although in some studies the authors have vaguely alluded to the notion of discourse, especially as related to the role of literature in the FLC, the potential for learning more about the overall interaction, cognition, discourse, and FLCs has not been fully realized. In addition, those studies mentioned earlier that do address authentic text and literature in the L2 classroom promote the value of the various readings as cultural rather than cognitive.

Kramsch writes that authentic texts and literature are used to present the product that instructors feel is most valuable to the students—culture: "Literary texts continue to be taught as finished products, to be unilaterally decoded, analyzed and explained" (1985, 356). Kramsch alludes to the type of classroom talk that is to be expected when dealing with literature in a FLC. The focus of the studies, however, is on the authentic text and literature, not the classroom talk that surrounds the literature.

Ricouer begins to focus on discourse processes, and not the explicit role of the text: "We need a methodology that fosters interpretation of the literary text as a dialectic process by which the reader surpasses both expla-

nation and understanding and appropriates the text" (1976, 74). This appropriation of the text is not easily defined, but as we can see, Ricouer is
concerned with how literature is perceived and how that perception affects
classroom talk and discourse. Kramsch and Ricouer do share some basic
similarities in their approach to the use of written text in a FLC; that is,
they both see the role of the literature as producing discourse and not
reproducing the text itself, or the culture it is representing.

In attempting to understand what Ricouer means by "appropriation,"
Kramsch (1985) offers the following in which the distinction is made between explanation and understanding—two concepts, which, in the FLC
may seem to be one and the same, but they play different roles when reading
and teaching literature:

Explanation is more directed towards the analytic structure of the text, understanding is more directed towards the intentional unity of discourse. [That is to say]
that the teacher can explain and teach the rhetorical structure, the form and content
of the text, but an understanding of the values, intentions, and beliefs embedded
in the text can only be achieved through open discussion and negotiation of meanings. According to Ricouer (1976) interpretation is a dialectic dynamic process by
which the reader surpasses both explanation and understanding and "appropriates"
the text for himself. (357)

Understanding that appropriation of the text comes by discussing the
text is central to investigating opportunities to enter into such discourse.
Analyzing literature, according to current thought, does not lead to appropriation of meaning through discourse. Opportunities to enter into negotiation discourse that are realized through the literature by the instructor
or students have not been addressed in the area of classroom-based research.

Frye sums up the complexity of appropriation by offering the following
interpretation of literature in the FLC: "The reader is a whole of which the
text is a part; the text is a whole of which the reader is a part" (1984, 56).
It is important to note that Frye sees the reader and the text as forming a
whole that is often divided because the role of the literature in the FLC is
ultimately to be reproduced through classroom interaction. According to
the research mentioned earlier, a goal of using literature in a FLC is to
reproduce the literature being studied. This then leads us to think about
the role that the foreign language plays in the classroom in relation to
discourse processes and opportunities for appropriation of the foreign language, and also for appropriation of cognitive skills. The combination of

text, language, and cognition in a literature-based FLC will benefit from further investigation and analysis.

## DYNAMIC FUNCTIONS IN THE CLASSROOM

The realm of teaching authentic texts and literature is a complicated one. However, when adding the element of learning a foreign language, the role of the instructor must address establishing necessary opportunities for the students to be exposed to the literature and to acquire and improve their L2 proficiency and skills.

Language use in a literature-based FLC has a variety of specific functions. Fillmore condenses these functions into two:

- To convey the information of what is to be learned: concepts and facts, language use in context, and information about the language itself
- To provide opportunities for students to receive linguistic input and to generate linguistic output in order to acquire a second language (1982, 43)

Realizing that these functions are very dynamic when understood through sociocultural lenses helps us to understand that language revolves around the goals set by the context and those speaking. In a FLC, the role of discourse is not as easily realized because we forget to include the human factor of cognition, understanding, and knowledge.

## THE MIND

Within a sociocultural framework, the mind extends beyond a person and people. The mind, according to Bateson (1972) and Geertz (1973), is socially distributed. That is, our mental habits and functioning are dependent on our interaction and communication with others, which are also affected by our environment, context, and history. Within each individual mind, there is mental action, which is then mediated socially by tools. These tools allow for individual minds to create and recreate their surroundings with language. Luria further clarified the notion of a socially mediated mind when he wrote: "In order to explain the highly complex forms of human consciousness one must go beyond the human organism. One must seek the origins of conscious activity and 'categorical' behavior not in the recesses of the human brain, but in the external conditions of life. Above all, this means that one must seek origins in the external processes of social life, in the social and historical forms of human existence" (1981, 21). This statement is important in understanding how in a FLC an individual student relies on more than just the teacher and him- or herself. Language is viewed as the primary tool in the FLC as it develops between individuals first then within individuals. As Vygotsky comments: "Any function . . . appears twice, or on two planes. First it appears on the social plane then on the psychological plane. First it appears between people as an interpsychological category, and then within the child as an intrapsychological category" (1981, 163). This appearance, then, is aided by the use of tools.

## TOOLS

Tools assist the developing communicative and cognitive functions in moving from the social plane to the psychological plane, or as Vygotsky states: from the interpsychological to the intrapsychological (1978). Volosinov depicts tools as such: "A tool by itself is devoid of any special meaning; it commands any designated function—to serve this or that purpose in production. The tool that serves [a] purpose as the particular, given thing that it is, without reflecting or standing for anything else" (1973, 10). The purpose of language is goal oriented toward either an activity or an understanding. This notion carries with it one of the purposes of language in a FLC: production of written and spoken language, and the production of understanding and of opportunities. The tool in the FLC is language that assists in mediating the discourse and activity of those involved in using tools. Tools are outward oriented, as opposed to signs, which are inward oriented, and affect both the user and the focus of their use. An important point to make is that with the introduction of language into an existing discourse, the tools may and often do change the ensuing actions. And, although tools are external, they are internally oriented as Vygotsky notes when he writes about psychological tools assisting the development of lower mental functions into higher mental functions: "In the instrumental act, humans master themselves from the outside—through psychological tools" (1978, 15). In other words, the constructive principle of the higher mental functions lies outside the individual—in psychological tools and interpersonal relations. These tools then assist in the creation and use of signs within the individual and the group.

Vygotsky's higher mental functions (such as summarizing, analyzing, and evaluating) are similar to those that Bloom (1956) incorporates into his taxonomy of cognitive functions, and in turn appear in Givens's FTCB (1976). Throughout these various methods of categorizing cognitive functions and skills, one element remains the same: language is understood as the main tool that assists individuals in obtaining the higher mental functions and cognitive skills.

Viewing our students in light that allows them to make use of the tools that they have available to them takes some of the pressure off of the instructor inasmuch as the instructor now can place part of the responsibility for negotiation of meaning and learning on the students. Too often has this tool metaphor been used to describe only teachers. That is, if we have the "right tools" then we can teach effectively. In part, this is correct, but it is essential that students are being exposed to new tools every day in our classes through texts and discussions or by listening. And as part of this shared responsibility, we need to allow students to put the tools into action to mediate their surroundings in whatever ways they choose.

What is important in understanding the concept of tools is that they are used during the process of classroom talk more for than a product. Products are what each one of us has in mind when we speak to each other. The process of tool use comes into play when we interact with each other in order to explain our viewpoints. But tools may first change or affect students intrapersonally before they may be able to express what they understand interpersonally.

Although some teachers may create a list of tools for their students to use and label them as agreeing, convincing, or rejecting an opinion, there is an element that the teacher does not see in those examples (and like them). They are treating language as a product instead of as a process. As such, linguistics is seen as more of a product under our current framework, and language (utterance, dialogue, and discourse) as a process.

## SIGNS

Signs are multifunctional tools of communication and representation. Signs, according to Volosinov (1973), carry with them certain ideologies that may be recreated and changed according to the situation and those present. Words, and even language itself, are devoid of meaning. It is when language is placed into a social situation that signs and, hence, ideologies are created internally through external experience, which is mediated by and through tools. In a FLC, words can be defined or given their equivalents (casa = house), but this falls short of language learning goals. Language does not hinge on memorizing vocabulary. After given the "tool" of "casa," a student can ask where another person lives, what his or her house is like, and a myriad of questions that lead to a development of the sign "casa" in the current social situation (not all houses or homes are alike if we think of family structure and physical traits, especially if we think about cross-cultural differences). Todorov writes: "The sign is described as something which refers back to something else, and may mediate social discourse" (1984, 18). In signs, meaning is created and reinforced or changed according to the given situation.

This concept is crucial to understanding sociocultural thought and those teachers who apply the true meaning of signs, as stated earlier, create a classroom where words are not defined, but understood in context. "Casa" is not a house, but where a certain character may feel safe and protected, such as a park or a restaurant. Those instructors that focus on the lexicon in order to build discourse will often fall into the IRE pattern of classroom talk where understanding is based on diction rather than fiction.

A sign refers to something else. This point is worth repeating. Just like we are "explained" by our relationships to those around us, so can a sign. In certain contexts, we are teachers where students are referred to us; in others we are sons or daughters where we are referred to our parents. It is not sufficient to give a name, a word, like "Harry," "Isabel," or "Mila." We must be able to see what it refers to, and so must our students.

## MEANING

Meaning within a sociocultural framework hinges on the use of signs. Given the occurrence of signs in a FLC, however, their meanings may or may not be reinforced by the instructor or the class. Halliday acknowledges the importance of reinforcement of meaning and signs when learning a language: "[Whatever] the child means, the message that gets across is one which makes sense and is translatable into the terms of the adult language" (1975, 24). We begin to develop an understanding for the role of the teacher in the FLC as one who interprets and reinforces meaning, but this role is not new. Students may also take on the role of interpreters and reinforcers of meaning in the FLC. Halliday's view, as Wells explains, is "not very different from Vygotsky's general account of the way in which participation in cultural practices leads to modification and transformation of the individual human's natural functions" (1999, 17). Meaning and signs in a FLC are socially introduced, reinforced, transformed, or modified through dialogue and discourse.

## SOCIAL SPEECH

It is necessary to point out the two functions of social speech that stem from and turn into dialogue and discourse. Vygotsky (1978) divides social speech into two functions. One function is that of communication with others. The other function is labeled as egocentric speech, which then leads to inner speech. Egocentric speech has also been called private speech (Wertsch 1991), been believed to steadily turn into inner speech, or "thought" as one is able to regulate one's own behavior (Lantolf and Appel 1994). Vygotsky clarifies the function of private speech by stating that: "The acquisition of language can provide an entire paradigm for the problem of the relation between learning and development. Language arises initially as a means of communication between [people] and [their] environment. Only subsequently, upon conversion to internal speech does it come to organize . . . thought, that is become an internal mental function" (1978, 89).

## ONGOING DISCOURSE

The framework of discourse is the next necessary step and is explained by Bereiter: "Classroom discussions may be thought of as part of the larger ongoing discourse. The fact that classroom discourse is unlikely to come up with ideas that advance the larger discourse in no way disqualifies it. The important thing is that the local discourses be progressive in the sense that understandings are being generated that are new to the local participants" (1994, 9). This statement and its application in the FLC are very important. Students may enter a FLC feeling as if what they talk about and how they talk does not matter outside the classroom where the language is being spoken. This, of course, is self-defeating. The central word from the previous quote is "progressive." Progressive discourse, as explained by Wells (1999), includes students involved in such tasks as agreeing, disagreeing, adding, revising, and clarifying. What is important is that students and teachers move beyond the "utterance" stage of communication and build on their dialogues. Dialogue helps create discourse that assists in learning a L2.

In order to exemplify what is meant by "discourse" in this study, I need to take a close look at an excerpt from a literature-based English as a FLC provided by Johnson as *The Diary of Anne Frank* is discussed:

**T = Teacher**

1. T: . . . and not only did he make them in one part of the city but when he started making them wear these yellow stars, I'll show you what that star looked like, it's called the Star of David, and it looks like this. (draws on board)
2. Tanzi: What does star mean?

3. T: What does this star mean?

4. Yuko: It's in the sky.

5. Tanzi: I know, but what does that mean?

6. T: Oh, what did it mean . . . what did it symbolize?

7. Tanzi: Yeah, symboli . . . ?

8. T: What did it symbolize? What did it stand for? . . . when you saw that star what did you think of?

9. Tanzi: Yeah, what, symboli . . . ? What did it . . . ?

10. T: What did it symbolize?

11. Tanzi: What did it . . . ?

12. T: Symbolize, what did it symbolize? OK, for the Jews it symbolizes David—one of their religious leaders—and for the Jews this star is a symbol of their belief in their religion.

13. Tanzi: It symboli . . .

14. T: Symbolizes

15. Tanzi: It symbolizes Jew religion?

16. T: Yes, it symbolizes the Jewish religion. And Hitler made all of the Jewish people wear a yellow star on their clothing, so everywhere they went, people knew they were Jewish . . . and Hitler wanted his people to blame the Jews for all the problems they were having at the time.

17. Tanzi: Anne, Anne Frank was . . . ?

18. T: Anne Frank was a Jew.

19. Tanzi: Anne Frank was a Jew?

20. T: Yes, Anne Frank was a Jew.

21. Tanzi: She had a yellow star?

22. T: Yes, she had to wear a yellow star.

23. Tanzi: Oh, she had to wear a yellow star? Oh, no . . . I wouldn't wear a star . . . I just wouldn't tell anyone.

24. T: So you wouldn't wear a yellow star? If you were Anne Frank you wouldn't wear a yellow star?

25. Tanzi: No. If I were her I wouldn't . . . I would run away.

26. T: If you were Anne Frank, you would run away?

27. Tanzi: If I were her, I would run away and they wouldn't find me . . . I don't know, it makes me scared a little bit . . .

28. T: Do you think Anne Frank was scared?
29. Tanzi: Yeah, if I were her, I think I would be scared, I think she was a little bit scared.
30. Yuko: But she had to wear it.
31. Tanzi: No, I wouldn't . . . I would hide like Anne Frank, I would run away . . .
32. T: What would you do, Yuko? If you were Anne Frank?
33. Yuko: I don't know, maybe if I were her, I would have to wear it. My parent would say I have to.
34. Tanzi: No, my parents wouldn't, they wouldn't wear it, we wouldn't wear it.
35. T: How do you think Anne Frank's parents felt about it?
36. Yuko: Maybe they get in trouble if they don't, so they have to wear it.
37. Tanzi: Maybe they have to, but I wouldn't, I wouldn't care, I just wouldn't wear it. (1995, 77–79)

This excerpt, although involving younger students, shows how an instructor can take advantage of the opportunities presented in the classroom to move beyond the dialogic realm, as in turns 1–22, and into discourse, from turns 22–37. These turns exemplify discourse because the teacher and the students are using information clarified before in turns 1–22 to move beyond the "word" (symbolize) and into what the actual students think and their own opinions. The instructor, in the following turns (30–37), asks the students about Anne Frank's parents and how they may have felt. Also, the instructor asks the students to put themselves into the place of Anne Frank. These two scenarios have no specific or "correct" answer. The instructor is attempting to have students use the language they have learned while using literature as a cognitive springboard for discourse.

Volosinov presents us with a more philosophical view of discourse:

Discourse (as all signs are) is generally interindividual. All that is said, expressed, is outside the "soul" of the speaker and does not belong to him only. But discourse cannot be attributed to the speaker alone. The author (the speaker) may have inalienable rights to the discourse, but so does the listener, to those whose voices resonate in the words found by the author (since there are no words that do not belong to someone). Discourse is a three-role drama (it is not a duet, but a trio). It is played outside the author, and it is inadmissible to inject it within the author. (1973, 300–301)

Brown and Yule summarize "discourse" as "text interpreted in context" (1983, 57). If we read again the turns from the two students (Tanzi and Yuko), we can see exactly what Brown and Yule mean. The students are interpreting the text according to their own insights and beliefs. More importantly, the instructor is taking advantage of the discourse opportunities for this to happen.

## VERBAL SCAFFOLDING

Given the linguistic background of students in a FLC, an immediate move into discourse may not always be possible because of linguistic or conceptual constraints or limitations. As such, it is important for instructors to use dialogue as a verbal scaffold into discourse. A clear example of verbal scaffolding by an instructor is provided in the following excerpt, which forms part of the ongoing classroom discourse. Johnson (1995) notes that in turns 2–16 the instructor is assisting Tanzi in appropriating and understanding the word "symbolize."

2. Tanzi: What does star mean?

3. T: What does this star mean?

4. Yuko: It's in the sky.

5. Tanzi: I know, but what does that mean?

6. T: Oh, what did it mean . . . what did it symbolize?

7. Tanzi: Yeah, symboli . . . ?

8. T: What did it symbolize? What did it stand for? . . . when you saw that star what did you think of?

10. Tanzi: Yeah, what, symboli . . . ? What did it . . . ?

11. T: What did it symbolize?

12. Tanzi: What did it . . . ?

13. T: Symbolize, what did it symbolize? OK, for the Jews it symbolizes David—one of their religious leaders—and for Jews this star is a symbol of their belief in their religion.

14. Tanzi: It symboli . . .

15. T: Symbolizes

16. Tanzi: It symbolizes Jew religion? (77–79)

By the end of this excerpt, Tanzi is able to reformulate the question by using the word "symbolize" appropriately. This verbal scaffold is made use of when the teacher asks the students what they would feel or do if they were made to wear the yellow star that symbolized Jews. Clearly, this verbal scaffold made it more possible for classroom talk to evolve into discourse.

Assistance by verbal scaffolding can also be given by students in the class (Donato 1994; Brooks and Donato 1994) to other students. The importance of verbal scaffolding becomes apparent when the classroom talk moves beyond the dialogic level and into discourse.

## RAILROADING AND SCAFFOLDING

Scaffolding has become another buzzword in our educational arenas, and when this does happen, unfortunately and ironically, it loses some of its original meaning and intention. Instructors may believe that their classes allow for scaffolding, and this may be true, but it is not the process that is under scrutiny, rather it is the goal or reason for scaffolding. Scaffolding our students to reach our own personal understanding of a piece of writing, without giving them the opportunities to reach their own conclusions, taints the underlying reasons for scaffolding. Remember that the context in which we are placing scaffolding is in a literature-based FLC. This context is very different from a first-year FLC. Scaffolding may occur for many linguistic or grammatical reasons, but the scaffolding that concerns me here is conceptual and cognitive in nature.

In the literature-based FLC, scaffolding has been misunderstood to mean and imply the idea of how to have students understand what the instructor has in mind. And this is only one-half of the equation. Scaffolding is not a one-sided phenomenon. If true scaffolding is to occur in literature-based FLC, then mutual understanding of each other's interpretation must be the goal. Moving toward only one interpretation has more in common with the concept of railroading than scaffolding. In railroading, the student is seen as an important part of interpretation, but the proper interpretation has already been set as the end goal. Student and instructor move alongside each other, laying tracks to a predetermined location. Those that build the tracks the fastest usually "do better in class," those that decide to explore their surroundings are often described as off-track. A track implies a goal, and the goal is more than likely set by the instructor when students read. Interestingly, if we picture a real-life scaffold alongside a building, and then imagine it from above after it has fallen down, it resembles a train track.

## COHERENCE AND COHESION

Understanding the difference between discourse coherence and discourse cohesion plays an important role in helping to recognize and form discourse within the literature-based FLC. Coulthard states that "the relation between [utterances] are aspects of grammatical cohesion" (1977, 10). He offers the following example:

A: Can you go to Edinborough tomorrow?
B: Yes, I can. (10)

According to Coulthard, it is the grammatical link of the word "can" that facilitates discourse coherence.

Discourse cohesion is rhetorically linked, according to Coulthard, and falls into the category of appropriate or inappropriate, according to the context. He offers this example of discourse cohesion:

A: Can you go to Edinborough tomorrow?
B: The (airline) pilots are on strike. (1977, 10)

B's answer requires that A have some background knowledge (that there is an airline strike). Although B's utterance is grammatically correct, without cohesion there is no discourse.

In a FLC, coherence and cohesion are important but have different roles. Coherence may be an end unto itself: "Just say it right." Cohesion may be more difficult to achieve because it does not rely on grammar only, but on interpretation, meaning, response, and context.

Discourse in the FLC builds on understanding that has come to exist over time and in various situations with both the students and the teachers acting as speakers and listeners throughout communication. All discourse has meaning embedded into it by the utterances of the participants.

## MEANING POTENTIAL

Rommetveit (1979a, 1979b) writes that in the processes of creating meaning we come into contact with words, either written or spoken. Part of learning another language, then, is becoming aware of when to use a word in dialogue. Each word spoken or written carries with it the task of having to be interpreted, and with this task also comes the semiotic baggage of meaning. The word or utterance in a FLC, much like in society, will be weighed and assigned meaning by the participants before being responded to. The idea of words carrying with them a meaning potential underlies the importance of everyone being involved in the discourse and that the speaker's intentions for or of a certain meaning do not always create the desired meaning in context.

Halliday suggests the following approach to the understanding of meaning potential: "The [linguistic] system is a meaning potential, which is actualized in the form of text; a text is an instance of social meaning in a particular context of situation. We shall therefore expect to find the situation embodied or enshrined in the text, not piecemeal, but in a way which reflects the systematic relation between the semantic structure and the social environment" (1978, 141). Based on this description of meaning potential, change is inevitable and the social reality of the foreign language in and out of the classroom is created and recreated daily. Todorov affirms the place of others in the creation of meaning: "Meaning [communication] implies community. Concretely, one always addresses someone, and that someone does not always assume a purely passive role (as the term 'recipient' would lead one to infer), the interlocutor participates in the formation of the meaning of the utterance, just as the other elements, similarly social, of the context of uttering do" (1984, 30). Halliday brings to light the concept of text. A clear understanding of text and its place in discourse in the FLC is essential to understanding the sociocultural framework.

The notion of text, although central to the general theme of this investigation, is viewed in a more supporting role. As stated earlier, meaning gives birth to negotiation and from there, discourse. This discourse allows us, and our students, to explore the limits of understanding (of which there may not be any) with the participants. If we begin to place meaning in its rightful category, fluid and dynamic discourse evolves. One point to make clear is that the meaning of which we speak, the meaning that creates or impedes opportunities for cognition, is not always lexical in its constitution. A car, by its very nature, will always be a car; its internal semantic properties dictate that it be so. It is when the notion, concept, or idea of "car" is challenged or used in an unfamiliar setting that negotiation is necessary and the potential for discourse is observed.

For example, envision a classroom setting where an instructor sets about introducing the term "slavery." This word can be defined to the satisfaction of both the students and the teacher. However, when placed into a dialogue, its meaning potential may grow exponentially. The difference is seen in the following sentence: We are slaves to our cars. The use of the word "slaves" supposedly brings about the notion of two entities in a warped relationship: one is the dominant and controlling master and the other submissive and powerless. In this simple sentence—we are slaves to our cars—there is meaning, but there is also much more meaning potential. It is this meaning potential that we have to take advantage of in our classes. What if a student disagrees? What if students begin to talk about other contemporary items that they believe to dominate our society, such as television and technology? Do we hold fast to our own professorial interpretations of slavery or do we try to use the concept to bring forth discourse and understanding through the L2? The answer is one that encompasses this present work and may be stated in the form of a question itself: In which class would you (as a student or teacher) rather take part?

## PRODUCT AND PROCESS OF TEXT

According to Halliday (1978), "text" includes both a product and process within a specific setting. Noting that the idea of text as a process and not just a product of discourse in a literature-based FLC is incorporated into the sociocultural framework will help clarify the roles of teachers and students in such classes. Also for Halliday (1978), the role of text in the FLC assists in building meaning throughout the discourse and it is not just a source of meaning that is presented to the students without further interpretation.

Bakhtin (1981) sees the role of text as working within dialogue to create a discourse. This discourse assists in mediating meaning throughout communication. As people, Bakhtin believes that we are given a certain reality by text: "The text, written or oral, is the primary datum of all these disciplines (linguistics, philology, literary studies). . . . The text is immediate reality (reality of thought and of experience) within which this thought and these disciplines can exclusively constitute themselves. Where there is no text there is no object of inquiry or thought" (1984, 17). This reality is developed in the FLC by the instructor, but is shaped by the students, a reality that, knowingly or not, is based on a text that is always being interpreted and reinterpreted. Todorov takes Bakhtin's thoughts on "text" and expands them further by comparing and contrasting them to the "language":

Every system of signs (that is, every "language"), no matter how limited the collectivity that adopts it by convention, can always be, in principle, deciphered; that is, translated into other sign systems (other languages); therefore, there exists a general logic of sign systems, a language of languages, potential and unified (obviously it can never become a particular concrete language, a language among others). A text (as distinct from language as a system of means) however, can never be fully translated, because there is no text of texts, potential and unified. (1984, 284–285)

If there is no one text to which we refer in order to interpret or understand a particular text, then how "text" is treated or understood in the FLC should be very different from "language." Language has a definitive point of reference whereas the point of reference for "text" (as to this framework) is momentary and evolves within the discourse created by the students or the instructor.

Todorov thus separates, at least philosophically, "language" and "text," but they do belong to the same system of signs that produces individual and unique meaning, and therein lies the difficulty of communication and discourse in a literature-based FLC. Instructors depend on a fixed system (language) to build a progressive discourse by interpreting contexts and texts that are evolving and can or could mean anything given the situation.

Finally, "text" in a literature-based FLC should be seen, as Lotman (1988) would agree, as creating meaning as well as having meaning. Coming to an understanding with the text, given the previous framework, carries with it some important implications because it is this striving for intersubjectivity that greatly assists in building discourse.

## INTERSUBJECTIVITY

Wertsch (1998) defines the purpose of intersubjectivity as attaining the goal of a shared perspective through communication. This shared perspective builds on the meaning generated through dialogue in hopes of building discourse. Applying the notion of intersubjectivity in the FLC is difficult when taking into account everything that generates meaning. In an attempt to simplify the "architecture of intersubjectivity," Rommetveit offers the following insight: "The basic problem of human intersubjectivity becomes . . . a question concerning in what sense and under what conditions two persons who engage in a dialogue can transcend their different private worlds. And the linguistic basis for this enterprise, I shall argue, is not a fixed repertory of shared 'literal' meanings, but very general and partially negotiated drafts of contracts concerning categorization and attribution inherent in ordinary language" (1979b, 7).

The private worlds in a literature-based FLC are, obviously, brought about or into play by the language. But we must not make the mistake of assuming that in understanding the language that we understand the speaker. Instructors are charged with trying to mediate the "private worlds" of the students in order for them to learn a language and to learn and interpret the literature. Bakhtin adds to the overall importance of the process of intersubjectivity by incorporating the listener, the utterances, and the speech (communication) in his explanation of how we come to an "otherness":

The fact is that when the listener perceives and understands the meaning (the language meaning) of speech, he simultaneously takes an active, responsive attitude toward it. He either agrees or disagrees with it (completely or partially), augments it, applies it, prepares for its execution, and so on. And the listener adopts this responsive attitude for the entire duration of the process and understanding, from the very beginning, sometimes from the speaker's first word. Any understanding of live speech, of a live utterance is inherently responsive, although the degree of this activity varies extremely. Any understanding is imbued with response and necessarily elicits it in one form or another: the listener becomes the speaker. A passive understanding of the meaning of perceived speech is only an abstract aspect of the actual whole of active responsive understanding, which is then actualized in a subsequent response that is actually articulated. (1986, 68)

It is the "passive understanding" of speech and communication that an instructor has to be aware of in the classroom because through this understanding classroom and student discourse is affected, which in turn may affect how or how much of the foreign language is learned. Intersubjectivity forms part of the foundation of sociocultural thought because the processes, being mediated by signs and tools, are dependent on the opportunities to enter into dialogue and discourse.

## OPPORTUNITIES

When speaking of opportunities, one automatically asks the question: Opportunities to do what? Within this framework, the focus will be on opportunities to engage in discourse (beyond the dialogue level or the initiation, response, and follow-up/evaluation [IRF/E] sequence). Another question arises when thinking of who provides these opportunities to enter into a classroom discourse using literature as the springboard or centerpiece for discussion. Understandably, both the instructor and students are capable of providing these opportunities in the literature-based FLC. The students are capable of initiating a dialogue, which may in response turn into a discourse on a particular topic and include communication with other students and/or the instructor. Discourse, for the purposes of this framework, does not revolve around the clarification or defining of a term or word. Rather, discourse is conceptually based and requires that those involved come to an understanding of what they believe to be the concept being discussed. Clarification of terms and definitions may lead into discourse about a related concept, but we must keep in mind that one of the purposes of discourse—understanding—hinges on the opportunities offered in the FLC allowing for contributions from other students or the instructor (Wells 1999).

As instructors, our students are evaluated based on their ability to take advantage of opportunities to show that they understand, and this is where we may falter. Realistically, in academic settings, evaluation of our students' progress and understanding (linguistic or not) has to be made. There are certain facts that our students have to know—such as the time period in which a piece of literature was written, the author's life, and other works that may have influenced the piece—that will assist them in reaching their goals. However, opportunities, as stated before, allow for contributions to overall understanding and for personal reflection.

Opportunities to engage ourselves in discourse for the purpose of building cognitive and linguistic abilities provide us with a wide array of topics and avenues when deciding how to initially approach a text. If we are aware of these opportunities, and the goals to which they may lead, then evaluation is more progressive and dynamic.

## UNDERSTANDING

Understanding through discourse involves a certain degree of coherence. Britton explains how this coherence through each level of classroom talk (utterance, dialogue, and discourse) is dynamic and progressive throughout the conversation:

[Understanding] is a function of the way in which the "utterance" is actually shaped, in the moment, to fit the demands of a particular activity in which one is engaged. In order to contribute in a progressive manner to the ongoing dialogue, one has to interpret the preceding contribution in terms of the information it introduces as well as of the speaker's [understanding] to that information, compare that with one's own current understanding of the issue under of the discussion and then formulate a contribution that will . . . add to the common understanding achieved in the discourse so far, by extending, questioning or qualifying what has already been said. (1982, 104)

By working toward an understanding through discourse, opportunities may prove to be central in providing others with talk that will assist in producing meaning through goal-directed action in the classroom.

# CHAPTER 5

❦

# *Control of Language and Ideas*

Instructors are charged with keeping a certain degree of control in any classroom environment. And in a L2 classroom, that control can be even more powerful because we are not only the linguistic experts, but also the conceptual mentors of the exchanges that take place in our classrooms. Almost everything that we do evolves into a pattern, for better or worse. But as educators and professionals, we need to take a look at these patterns in order to try to improve our teaching and the students' learning. These patterns emerge and are not arbitrary. Although our decisions are not always conscious ones, they are still decisions that are based on experiences, inter- actions, and reactions.

## TRADITIONAL CLASSROOM DIALOGUE

In order to help define what is considered discourse in a FLC, it is necessary to take a look at traditional classroom dialogue that has been outlined by Lemke (1985, 1990a) as consisting as of three basic moves: initiation, response, and follow-up/evaluation (IRF/E sequence). This type of interaction has been shown by Lemke to consist of 70 percent of all classroom interaction that he studied in secondary schools. According to Wood (1992), the teacher asks too many questions of the "answer-known" variety and does not allow for the student to take on the role of initiator in class "discussions." Lemke (1990a) criticizes the triadic dialogue (i.e., the IRE sequence) found in classrooms because on the surface students seem to be participating more, and the IRE sequence may encourage maximum student participation in a teacher-fronted classroom.

It is a mistake to think that this type of pattern of classroom talk only happens in "lower level" FLCs. As we shall see later, the IRE sequence has a strong presence in the patterns of communication in a literature-based FLC. This presence, often misunderstood for discourse, fosters the patterns of talk and interaction that instructors believe to be "discourse." Viewing discourse beyond the present evaluative IRE sequence places more of the burden on the instructor to use the IRE sequence for a purpose, rather than to just railroad students into only one interpretation. The IRE sequence, if nothing else, is comfortable. It provides a framework for interaction in a language that is not our own in a L2 classroom. This said, then what needs to be pointed out is the necessity to focus on what we may call our own in the event our cultural and linguistic egos take hold of our self-perceptions: our thoughts and our reactions. As instructors, we value inter-action, of which the IRE sequence provides the initial impetus, and realistically we have to make sure that the basic facts of a story are clear (it may take place in a king's castle as opposed to a monastery). This should not be construed as an argument against the IRE sequence, but rather just the opposite. It is an argument for using it appropriately. After making sure that all of students understand the basics of the work that is being read (e.g., the setting, characters, and plot), interpretation takes hold of our cognitive domains while our linguistic skills are placed into play to try to express those domains.

## PATTERNS OF CLASSROOM COMMUNICATION

Johnson (1995) makes a very interesting point when she writes that patterns of classroom communication are not random because instructors establish and maintain patterns of communication by the use of task structure, content, and language. Instructors hold certain assumptions about what their classes will resemble and do. Establishing patterns of communication is not necessarily a negative aspect of the FLC. If certain patterns of communication lead the students to certain goals, then the pedagogical aspects of the methodology are carried out by task completion. Trueba (1989) also understands that patterns of classroom communication exist, but believes that in order for students to be given the greatest number of opportunities for discourse patterns must vary in order for them to participate and learn the language and the content. The IRE sequence may serve a purpose, but once the purpose is served (e.g., establishing the main characters of a novel) instructors stay with and rely on the IRE sequence because of their limited expectations and views of the students in their classes (Carrasco 1981). If students interpret the expectations of the instructor as such, then classroom patterns of communication will be set by both the teachers and students, perhaps by not allowing students to give or present opportunities for discourse because the teachers believe that "it is not how the class is taught" (Hymes 1981). Patterns of communication may constrain, inhibit, or enhance discourse and opportunities for discourse in the FLC.

## ROLE OF THE INSTRUCTOR

The role of the instructor in the literature-based FLC is not easily defined. On the one hand, instructors are charged with presenting the literature and authors in such a way that their students will be readily equipped to understand the various historical literary movements and styles. On the other hand, instructors are also charged with helping students refine not only their cognitive abilities, but linguistic ones as well. So, a not-so-simple question rises from these roles: Can an instructor in a literature-based FLC help students acquire their L2 and to what degree? This may very well become an extension of this study after its completion. But first, I should focus on the complexity of the instructor's role.

As Steiner notes: "[The instructor] may find out that he is no longer a dispenser of information or a performer. He becomes an organizer, a writer, a diognostician, a counselor, and a teacher. Most teachers have had the potential to fulfill these various roles, but they have not had experience playing them" (1972, 280).

The keyword here is "experience." Without experiencing the various roles as a student, instructors then rely on those models they know best: their own teachers. And, most likely their own teachers understood FLCs to be reproductive environments where the students and teachers reproduce, through dialogue, the text being studied. If instructors are to assume various roles in the literature-based FLC, then the classroom must be seen and understood as a productive environment where ideas are shared through the target language.

Instructors may not feel comfortable guiding their students "linguistically" in the literature-based FLC because, after all, they are studying the literature, rather than the language. We can take into consideration Santoni's (1971) reflections on the use of linguistic guidance by the instructors (e.g., asking a question in the past tense to assist a student in using the same tense in the answer). Santoni writes: "Some may argue that such (a linguistic focus) will end intuition. On the contrary, control of language does not mean control of ideas" (435); and it may be this approach that we as instructors need to apply in the FLC.

Santoni's point deserves further attention and explanation. In an environment where language and literature are precariously balanced, instructors may tend to believe that they control the literature through the language being spoken in the classroom. Although to some extent this may be true (asking questions about the readings for which the teachers already know the answer) and since it is literature (supposedly) that is to learned, then we, as instructors, try to focus on controlling what is to be learned: literature. But as will be shown later in the analysis, what really ends up being controlled is the language and the discourse surrounding the literature. Perhaps, if instructors approach literature though discursive lenses, then students will feel more comfortable using their linguistic skills (which are being guided by the instructor) to explain and explore the text.

For example, we can see the types of questions that fall under these two approaches:

### Literature through language

Who is the main character of the story?

When is the story set?

Where does this work fit into the author's development?

What does "gallows" mean?

### Language through literature

Why do you think that the main character ran away from his family?

Would you have enjoyed living in the town where the book takes place? (Reasons for this . . . )

Which criminal would be most afraid of the gallows in this story? (Reasons for this . . . )

Interestingly, when reviewing the previous questions, the second set of questions have a much more "literary" feel to them. If we try to think of possible answers to all of the questions, then we can see the amount and type of language that is necessary to answer these. Also, if we take the teacher's role, the questions that would afford more opportunities for classroom talk and communication would be those in the second set. Understandably, a baseline or context has to be set and understood by the teacher and students, but what is crucial is that we move beyond the baseline and build on both the readings and the language.

Lemke (1985) writes about instructors exerting "thematic and interactional control" in language classrooms. Instructors in literature-based FLCs may have more of a challenge keeping thematic control if the interaction moves beyond the triadic discourse mentioned earlier. The control of the "theme" in the literature-based FLC may not seem problematic at first, but even though students may be reading a work of literature with "a theme," they cannot help but interpret it. This interpretation is what may shift the thematic control to the students.

## EXPECTATION AND INTERPRETATION

The two sides of classroom communication can be clearly divided into expectations and interpretations. Interestingly, the review of current research in the teaching of literature in the FLC addresses or assigns expectations to the instructor and interpretation to the students. Logically, we see that communication is the combination of both expectation and interpretation in understanding classroom talk. But what is not made clear is that in order for classroom talk to move beyond the IRE sequence or dialogue level, clarification of expectations and interpretations must occur within both the students and the teacher. Expectations should not be understood only as what is written on the syllabus, and interpretations should be open for discussion and exploration.

McCarthy sums up the complexity of the literature-based FLC and the role of the instructor: "What is called for at this level is [attempting to achieve] the hybrid goal of advanced language competence [and] increasing literary competence" (1998, 12).

As we shall see, the dichotomy between expectation and interpretation is also reflected in the curriculums and syllabi of courses. But what makes these even more precarious is that our goals within these syllabi are "material focused." That is to say, they may be used to present the literary works of a certain country, era, or literary movement. An obvious question arises from the previous statement: Then what should guide our courses? Cognitive skills? In a sense, the answer is yes. What is being proposed is not a return to the days of Socrates when thinking was the material that gave rise to substance. But in a curriculum-driven world where, at times, covering the material may take precedence, cognitive skills are seen as a natural by-product of the material. Is thinking solely a by-product of literature or is it necessary to think before producing or reading literature? Instead of placing cognition at one end or the other of this spectrum, it should be placed throughout the process of interacting with the text. If this is reflected in the courses and syllabi, then we need not change the materials or subjects taught, but only adjust our approach.

## EXPLORATORY TALK

McCarthy's (1998) goal may be achieved through what Vande Berg (1993) understands as offering two different types of questions: analytic and interpretive. Both of these types of questions have their uses in the FLC. According to Vande Berg, however, interpretive questions cause the most anxiety, so instructors may tend to rely on more analytical (answer-known variety) questions so as not to cause the students any unneeded stress. Lack of interpretive questions may cause students to use less exploratory talk, defined by Johnson as: "Generating ideas [at the same time] as they [the students] participate in negotiation of meaning as they reached a consensus about the specific question they wanted to ask. Moreover, [students using exploratory talk] were allowed to select the topic of discussion [within the theme], overlap talk, control the direction of discussion, and self-select [volunteer] when and how to participate" (1995, 151).

The area of "exploratory talk" and discourse in the literature-based FLC has not been fully investigated, and doing so will help to understand and clarify the nature of communication in a literature-based FLC.

## SUMMARY

There are an unlimited number of patterns of communication in a L2 classroom, just like in our daily lives. However, it is when an instructor falls into repeating a pattern that does not extend the thinking or language of the students that we have to begin to take a close look at the goals and objectives of the class. As we all know, teaching (and learning) is an endeavor that is at the very crux of our existence. However, at times we sacrifice the content of what is to be taught for the form.

That is to say that, as stated earlier, the content of language is thought and meaning. These depend on a dynamic and fluid (and somewhat guided) interaction in the classroom. It is when we break out of these prescribed patterns that we begin to really learn, teach, and think for ourselves.

# CHAPTER 6

∞

# *Affect and Literary Response*

I have yet to fully discuss the variables and elements of literary response in the FLC. Although, as mentioned before, few attempts have been made to link literary theory with L2 acquisition, if we venture into the realm of teaching literature in our "native language" classrooms (in this case, English) then there are various ideas and concepts from current literary theory that may assist in providing opportunities for discourse and engage students at higher cognitive levels. Frye (1970) makes the interesting remark that what is really being taught in our literature classrooms is literary criticism and that the goal of teaching literature is rather futile. These ideas are rooted in the values placed on affect and personal experience when approaching literature in the classroom. Before the term "diversity in being" was offered in hopes of providing an outlook that when we teach literature it is not just understanding that is shaped by the students' reading, but also that the students themselves may have reassessed their own viewpoints, and in effect adapted or changed, intrinsically, in the process.

## FIELD OF PLAY

Pertosky (1992) frames the literature classroom and our students in what he calls a "field of play." Within this field, the instructor attempts to offer opportunities to scaffold the students in order to provide students with food for thought, but here this "food" is taken and digested, and used by each student in very personal ways, not just taken to be regurgitated at a later point in the semester.

**Figure 6.1**
**Fields of Play**

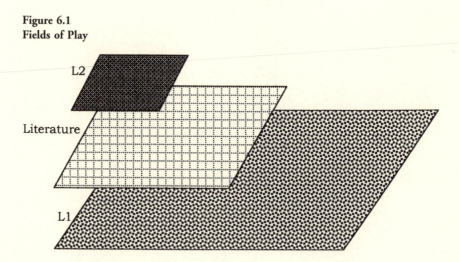

Our situation in the fields of SLA and foreign language education is further complicated by the fact that the students have become aware of another parallel field of play, one in which the foreign language to be learned defines the boundaries. Our task would be less complicated if the boundaries of these fields (literature and language) were similar as in the task of teaching literature in a "native language" setting as previously mentioned. But as it stands, we now have three fields of play, at least, to contend with: literature (reading), student's L1, and the particular language of the FLC. Figure 6.1 is a diagram of the three essential fields of play within each student (and instructor). Although separated in order to demonstrate the varying sizes of the fields, these are all one-in-the same and are rather dynamic. But if we take a look at the figure, what becomes clear is that in order for students in a FLC to take advantage of every field available to them, the approach one takes is critical. If we approach literature through L1, then we miss the benefits that literature affords SLA and the FLC. If we approach literature through L2, then there is a danger of not moving beyond the linguistics constraints of the field of play. Then, we need a common thread that helps us apply knowledge that we have from L1 into literature while using a L2. Perhaps this may seem a simple solution, but it is not an easy task.

Finding a common thread between the fields of play is a theoretical quest. This trip begins with the delineation of two useful theories and ends with a proposed amalgamation, or hybrid, that instructors in FLC may find useful.

## TEXT THEORY

Kintsch (1988), seeing that the current beliefs of how one understands literature needs revising, underlines the shortcomings of a top-down process to literary interpretation. The top-down processes, according to Kintsch, does not take into consideration that at times we do not have the sufficient schemata needed to fully benefit from the text. He then proposes that readings should be seen and approached though a bottom-up point of reference as well in order to introduce the reader to the various stylistic differences in literary texts (Empson 1961).

The following are the basic elements of Kintsch's Text Theory adapted from Miall and Kuiken (1994):

Basic thesis: Style economizes comprehension

Exemplary texts: Minimal stylistic variation

Responses to style: Features are transformed into familiar concepts

Subjective emphasis: Discussion value

Mnemonic resources: General world knowledge

Integrative strategy: Building macropropositions

Outcome: Theme or gist

Reader differences: Incidental

From this outline, we can readily envision a class that is being taught with these concepts in mind. We should remember, though, that this framework is built around L1 literary response and teaching. On the surface, it seems quite applicable to almost any setting in which literature or readings are being discussed. As Miall and Kuiken (1994) note: In general, text theories describe a resource-limited system in which cognitive structures or procedures economize comprehension by deleting irrelevant propositions, inferring relevant propositions, and building macropropositions.

If we look closely, there is a pivotal factor that is missing: affect. This variable, when placed in the literary classroom and given its due focus, changes our approach as teachers and the experiences of our students.

## DEFAMILIARIZATION THEORY

This approach to understanding literary response has been championed in the past (Mukarovsky 1977; Van Dijk 1979) in order to provide a framework where response is guided by responses of the mind (affect) instead of by themes or propositions. As Shlosvsky (1965) expresses, literary texts hinge on the various stylistic devices that assist in augmenting the emotional effect on the readers. In other words, it is when we are not familiar with what we are reading, stylistically, conceptually, or contextually, that our responses may not be able to fit within the confines of the language that we know. So, it is important to have others around in order to help us put into words what we have experienced. The goal here is not to use someone else's words to talk about our experience, but to be able to interact and talk with others so that we flesh out our responses for others to understand. It is this fleshing out of concepts and reactions in a FLC that would benefit our linguistic and cognitive goals.

The following is an outline of the Defamiliarization Theory just reviewed:

Basic thesis: Style enriches comprehension

Exemplary texts: Maximum stylistic variation

Responses to style: Stylistic features provoke and engage feelings and concepts

Subjective emphasis: Personal response

Mnemonic resources: Personal memories and perspectives

Integrative strategy: Affective focus

Outcome: Alternative perspective on world and self

Reader differences: Fundamental

This outline differs greatly from the Text Theory, and its core is the reader's personal, or affective response, to the reading. Before, the suggestion was that we look for more than a difference in understanding from our students and that we also foster a difference in being. This outcome—difference in being—is contained within the previous framework where an outcome of the reading may be that students view themselves and their worlds differently, and therefore become different people than they were prior to reading the text.

However, the Defamiliarization Theory is constructed from L1 responses to texts in L1 classrooms. And as we all know, it is a large theoretical leap from an L1 to an L2 classroom. If we are to apply a literary theory to a L2 classroom, then we cannot take either the Text Theory or the Defamiliarization Theory "as is" and force it into and onto our students. The reality of foreign language education in the United States would not allow us to do so. But what can be done is to combine various elements into a more realistic, contemporary outlook that takes into account the text-focused nature of linguistic study in the FLC in the United States and that allows room for the foundations of cognition and affect.

## THREE-FIELDS THEORY

Pausing for a moment, the reader should return to the earlier argument and explanation centered on the three fields of play. The reader should remember that our students are incorporated, whether we want them to or not, into those three fields every time that we summon the use and voices of texts and authors to our L2 classrooms. The task was to find a common thread between the three fields of play: L1, L2, and literature. And that common thread is one that is made by using cognition, affect, and language in the following Three-Fields Theory:

Basic thesis: Style leads to comprehension and personal reaction

Exemplary texts: Stylistic variation is adjusted according to linguistic proficiency

Responses to style: Stylistic features are used to outline familiar concepts that in turn engage us in personal responses and assist in building new concepts

Mnemonic resources: Personal perspectives guided by general world knowledge

Integrative strategy: Building of discourse through affective responses

Outcome: Differences in understanding and being

Reader differences: Assist in defining any general themes and in providing opportunities for discourse

Taking the Text and Defamiliarization Theories and transforming them into the Three-Fields Theory assists us in applying a framework to our FLCs where we use literature and authentic materials (see Figure 6.2). This theory can also be easily translated into an approach (which may be the hallmark of a true theory) where students do not feel lost by wondering which field they are playing on now and where the instructor allows for discussion that may lead to the building of linguistic proficiency.

## WHY USE LITERATURE?

At times, we are faced with having to explain to our colleagues, parents, or students why the study of literature, by itself, is important. In order to do so, for the time being we need to remove it from the realm of foreign language education. This is not say that the following reasons support the

**Figure 6.2**
**Centering the Three Fields of Play in a FLC**

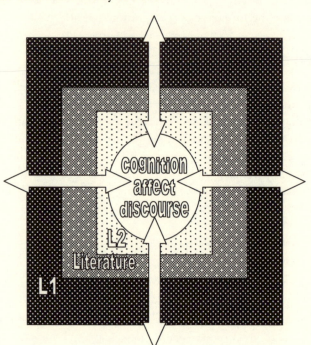

use of literature solely outside of the FLC. But in order to set the ground-work for approaching literature from a discourse and cognitive perspective in the language classroom, we must first understand the inherent value of literature when removed from educational settings, regardless of the language.

Initially, literature provides us with windows into the experiences that are beyond our realms. It allows us to become, in a manner of speaking, self-reflective. Not only do we interact with the literary text and create a world of our own, but we also compare the literary realm to our own, therefore making us more aware of our current surroundings. Our imagination is put into play. Worlds are created in our minds where words on a page become signs in our minds. Also, literature creates a type of stress between the reader and the text. We use our imaginations to strain the limits of the textual realm according to our own personal insights. This stress is not emotional, as in a nervous state, but within the realm of the literature and the reader limits are tested and finally delineated.

Literature is also a history of thought and thinking. Here is where many instructors impose their interpretations on their students in any classroom. This history, in the classroom, can be approached as whole because of the given contexts or time periods. It is when we take apart the history, piece by piece, that we have to be careful about constraining and imposing only one aspect that we believe to be essential to us.

## CULTURE AND LITERATURE

Literature cannot be separated from culture. We use literature to perform a global discourse within our communities and to convey information to those outside our environments about our beliefs, way of life, and elements of our daily lives. In this sense, literature belongs to the people—not just to those who wrote the text, but also to the groups and individuals who inspired the text and shaped it by being in contact with the author in one way or another. Within this aspect or approach, literature takes the symbols of our ethics and beliefs and transfers them into a cultural setting where imagination and personal environment shape affect and response. Through this window into literature, we can see ourselves as knights, spies, pirates, and presidents as we try to achieve an understanding of what the character must be going through in that particular culture of the text.

Literature also gives us a cultural anchor that we hold on to throughout our lives. The stories that our grandparents read to us and the books that our parents bought for us are culturally important to us because they help define who we are in history. Literature may help stereotype our cultures, and this is the basic danger that instructors have to be wary of in the FLC. As noted earlier, if we use literature in the classroom to help "experience precede expression," then the expression of our students should not be stereotyped or prototyped according to our own expressions and interpretations.

Literature can also be elitist. And unfortunately, it is this embodiment that some of us have encountered in our classes and discussions that has made us feel unable to understand the literature, as a cultural entity, rather than as a personal reflection. Using literature also helps to establish prominent ideas of the time that have no other interpretation but that of those who understood it to begin with, and this is where we begin to study interpretation instead of literature in our classrooms and where we may feel that we can impose our interpretation on a class or individual.

An elitist view of literature in a FLC produces a cultural dictatorship based on interpretations of interpretations. This may happen to the point where the culture that surrounded the literature disappears in a swamp of personal, almost acultural interpretations. Students know when an instructor is lecturing for the test. That is, students understand that the "correct answer" does not necessarily come from them, but from the instructor in a classroom that harbors literature as the realm of the elite. This view has a devastating effect on the patterns of classroom talk and discourse, as will be seen later in this investigation.

## SUMMARY

The two different boundaries that were described in this chapter—Text Theory and Defamiliarization Theory—were useful inasmuch as they provided the impetus for a more contemporary and practical theory of literature and reader response. Placed in the L2 classroom, the Three-Fields Theory allows the centerpiece (cognition, discourse, and affect) to hold together the three fields of L1, L2, and literature. As was argued, approaching literature in a L2 setting cannot be beneficial if the methodology is completely grounded in the approach to literature solely in the L1. Nor can it be beneficial if we approach literature solely from a linguistic point.

In short, we have misunderstood and narrowed the ways to approach literature in the L2 classroom in recent times. We need to reorganize our goals and objectives to encompass those that include and value the personal aspects of reading literature and to realize that these aspects can be turned into opportunities for discourse that may affect linguistic proficiency and cognitive abilities.

Literature is written to be thought of and to be imagined. These processes, within us, tend to be author or character specific. In other words, through the pages of literature we grasp someone else's experience and perhaps struggle with it if it is not familiar to us. But in the end, our minds are able to understand and "see" another world that is historical, fictional, or contemporary. In turn, this gives us reason for expression and thought. Literature also defines itself. If we read several pieces by the same author or written during the same era, then previous works and meanings may become better understood.

# CHAPTER 7

∽

# *Cognitive Construction*

There are numerous avenues that we can take when we try to understand the very nature of cognition, how it is linked to discourse, and how these links can be taken advantage of by students of a L2. However, students will need the guidance of instructors that understand the importance of discourse and opportunities to enter in various forms and patterns of exchanges in the L2. What follows is a pragmatic view of the patterns, goals, and implications of the ways cognition may be constructed in our classrooms.

## COCONSTRUCTION

By attempting to or actually reaching intersubjectivity, students coconstruct meaning as they share various perspectives according to their interpretations and experiences. This type of communication has been understood as "social interdependence" or has been addressed as a type of a "transitive" discourse (Tharp and Gallimore 1988), but one aspect of this type of communication is evident, as Forman and Cazden (1985) note: that by developing and working through the process of coconstructing meaning, that is, reaching intersubjectivity, students (and instructors) do benefit cognitively by engaging in such tasks or discourse.

Wells (1999) writes about what he considers to be the "sociocultural conception" of coconstruction and intersubjectivity. He later adds that the main goal of a classroom based on the sociocultural framework is the "creating and sustaining of a community of inquiry" (229). In an effort to provide instructors (and learners) with an outline of just how to create such a discourse and the various important parts, Wells defines the characteristics of what he calls the "Practice of Education,"

The activities undertaken are such that, although chosen by the teacher for their cumulative contribution to an understanding of the central theme, they allow for groups of students to make them their own, and progressively to exercise more choice over how they are conducted.

They involve a combination of action and reflection, and of group work, individual reading and writing, and whole-class discussion.

Goals are made explicit and the relationship between these goals and operations by means of which they are to be achieved is made the subject of discussion.

Perhaps most important, there are frequent opportunities to express their beliefs and opinions, to calibrate them with those of their peers, and to change them in the light of persuasive argument or of further information. (1999, 228)

Viewing instruction and communication, as outlined in the previous extract, we can more clearly understand the central role the creation of opportunities takes as the class engages in discourse. The students, in this type of environment, would benefit more cognitively (Engestrom 1991) and are also given more room to explore what they know about the area being discussed and are given an arena to learn a foreign language.

A community of inquiry includes the instructor. Here, the teacher, although very familiar with the material being taught, may not be familiar with the interpretations and reactions that the students will have. We are defined by the subjects that we teach, in this case L2s, and we find self-validation and recognition in describing ourselves as "French literature teachers" or "Spanish literature teachers," and rightfully so. To be able to understand a vast area of work, in any language, requires commitment and expertise. But as stated earlier, a community shares an understanding of a topic or subject through discourse, rather than through a label.

## HETEROGLOSSIA

When we are coming to terms with others through discourse, we may depend on the words or experiences that we have read about or heard. When we try to have our listeners understand us through others' words or experiences in the process of reaching intersubjectivity, we appropriate someone else's views. This appropriation of others' views and meanings is what Bakhtin calls "heteroglossia": "Prior to this moment of appropriation, the word does not exist in a neutral and impersonal language (it is not, after all, out of a dictionary that the speaker gets his words), but it exists in others people's mouths, in other people's concrete contexts, serving other people's intentions: it is from there that one must take the word and make it one's own" (1981, 293–294). Appropriation of words, at the basic level in a FLC, may come through utterances, but appropriation of meaning and understanding come through the process of discourse.

If we look back to the formation of the concept of dialogue mentioned earlier, we see that a dialogue involves three entities, one of which may be outside the speaker or listener. This "outside entity" (i.e., previous experience) comes to light as ventriloquism. As Bakhtin (1981) notes, we find the words that we use already "lived in" by the intentions and experiences of others. Volosinov (1978) believes that in order to truly understand each other, we must first find ways to "overcome the word" through discourse.

## ACTIVITY SETTING

Tharp and Gallimore (1988) define the classroom context of discourse as the activity setting. The activity setting is both fluid and concrete, where the instructor is responsible for providing support for communication: "The criterion for an educationally effective activity setting is that it should allow maximum assistance in the performance of tasks at hand. The activity setting is a unit of analysis that transcends individuals, and provides a meaningful way to integrate culture, local contexts, and individual function" (130).

Also, within the activity setting framework Rogoff and Wertsch (1984) lay out the foundation for interpreting discourse in a FLC as "emergent interactionism," where the competent speaker provides maximum support for communication with another. Within the activity setting, the instructor has the responsibility to provide opportunities for discourse and to establish goals within the framework of a FLC. Tharp and Gallimore stress the importance of having goals within discourse: "[These] goals are achieved through group discussions that create discourse meaning structures that are both intermental and intramental. The entire group of teacher and students shares both verbal language and written text, and so this is intermental, simultaneously, these meanings are internalized for each member and become part of the thought system of each individual" (1988, 132).

Discourse should assist students in reaching their own goals and the ones set out by the instructor as well. Trying to find a balance between directing toward a goal or just "letting go" to see where the classroom discussion might lead may be one of the areas in which instructors have difficulty deciding on specific frameworks for discussions.

## GOAL-DIRECTED ACTION

Lave (1977) identifies a similar concept to that of Tharp and Gallimore's (1988) activity setting, one he calls "arena." In this arena, tools and settings are joined by goals. Crucial to the understanding of Lave's arena is that how and when the mind develops depends on the tools that one has and develops through interacting in an activity setting. As one develops various and new tools, these in turn may also determine the goals that one chooses, and in turn assist in developing other tools. Within the idea of the arena and goal-directed action, Lave and Wegener (1991) help us understand that learning through discourse does not necessarily mean controlling the discourse itself or actively participating in it to any great extent. They use the term "legitimate peripheral participation" when referring to those students who may reach a goal though not actively participating in progressive discourse. As students become more comfortable with the goal and the discourse in the classroom, they become more overtly active in communication.

The linguistic goals in a FLC may be difficult to reach if the students are not able to interact and communicate in the target language. Understanding that via discourse one builds and discovers new tools that assist in cognitive development, we realize how the cognitive goals of a FLC can be met and put to use outside of the classroom. As Wells explains: "Classroom activities should not only lead students to construct a personal understanding of the topics involved that equips them to participate effectively and responsibly in similar and related activities beyond the classroom, but [they] should also encourage the development, disposition, and the necessary strategies to adopt the same stance independently in new and unfamiliar situations" (1999, 91).

In using the word "stance," Wells refers to a cognitive rather than a linguistic goal. As a clear goal, a discourse-driven classroom understands that discourse, although responsible for building linguistic knowledge of the foreign language, may also affect how students communicate in their L1 on similar topics. After all, psychological tools affect how a person chooses to communicate and not just in which language.

## SUMMARY

The previous concepts, when placed into practice, build on each other. As stated earlier, the goals of the classroom, if cognitive, will lend themselves to a more open, discourse-driven type of classroom talk. This envisioned classroom talk incorporates Wells's notions of the practice of education. Instructors should become aware of these concepts, but are to stop short of defining them for the students. "Lessons on heteroglossia" should not be overtly emphasized. Concepts such as these are for part of a larger process and are not products to be quantitatively measured. They are tools that we use to adjust, build, reshape, and develop cognition through language. And that may be why instructors feel a bit uneasy when asked to apply such a framework to their classrooms. These tools and this type of talk are not products that can be easily measured for evaluative purposes. In part, this is why in literature-based FLCs instructors tend to spend their time defining words (as will be shown later) and not talking about concepts. Words have a definition whereas concepts require understanding of meaning. Later in this text, the issue of grammar in a literature-based FLC will be addressed as well as an approach on how to view grammar in such an environment.

# CHAPTER 8

∞

# *Analyzing Cognition and Discourse*

This chapter outlines the methodology used for the data analysis for the present study. It also assists in further extending and building the socio-cultural theory of communication, discourse, and cognition (Wells 1999; Wertsch 1991; Vygotsky 1978) by presenting methods and instruments that are used in analyzing the text-centered talk (TCT) of the present course.

Of interest to this methodology is the concept of goal-directed action (Tharp and Gallimore 1988) because it is within this interaction between instructor, class, and individual students that the notions of intersubjectivity (Wertsch 1986), of a socially distributed mind (Bateson 1972), and of a mediated mind (Luria 1981) develop. The present methodology takes into account the various tools that language affords the participants to create dialogue and discourse while communicating.

A pilot study was completed before the present investigation. The pilot study was also centered around the SPN 3201 course.

## PILOT STUDY

Two SPN 3201 courses were observed, recorded, and analyzed according to the methodology set forth for this present study. Each of the courses for the pilot study was observed three times over a six-week period. Each course met for fifty minutes, three times a week, and all of the students were nonnative speakers of Spanish. The courses were taught by native speakers of Spanish. Both instructors held doctorate's in Hispanic literature.

The general purposes of the pilot study were:

- For the researcher to familiarize himself with the university-level FLC environment

- To practice and refine the use of the text-based talk analysis according to the levels of utterance, dialogue, and discourse

- To practice and refine the use of the FTCB in the analysis of students' responses

- To initially investigate the course that was to be the focus of the present study

The general findings of the pilot study were supported by the findings of the present study, whereas the majority of text-based talk was dialogue and 55 percent of the student responses were knowledge of specifics. During the classes observed for the pilot study, there was an emphasis on development of vocabulary (i.e., lexical linking). Also, the cognitive skills of analysis, synthesis, and evaluation were present 20 percent of the time during TCT.

Two basic steps were followed after the recorded classes were transcribed: (1) classroom talk was assigned a level of classroom talk: utterance, dialogue, and discourse; and (2) the responses of the students were coded by using the FTCB. Also, the use of an outside observer was implemented according to Lincoln and Guba's (1985) constructs for interrater reliability and trustworthiness.

This chapter assists in further extending and building the sociocultural theory of communication and discourse by presenting methods and instruments that were used in analyzing the TCT of the present course.

In order to examine the characteristics of classroom talk in a literature-based FLC, data for the study was collected through audiotapes of lessons, instructor interviews, and course syllabi, as well as the institution's course description. Qualitative and quantitative analysis of literature-based FLCs were used to examine the classroom talk.

Discourse analysis has proven an effective method of investigating how language patterns form and interactional processes influence classroom talk in a FLC (Allwright 1984; Cazden 1986; Johnson 1995; Wells 1999, 1993). Appel and Lantolf (1994), Donato (1994), and Tharp and Gallimore (1988) demonstrate through their own socioculturally based research that "social interaction" plays a crucial role in not only language development, but in cognitive development as well. Through discourse analysis, processes in which language acts as a psychological tool are better explained and defined. These, in turn, help us focus our methodologies in the classroom for better learning and educational opportunities.

## COURSE AND CLASS OBSERVED

As part of the agreement with the students and instructor of the course being observed: the university where the study took place has not been identified so as to afford the participants the comfort of interaction and participation in the classroom for this and future investigations, and as a professional courtesy that we traditionally extend to each other in our field of inquiry.

Spanish is one of fourteen languages offered at the university, and one of five languages in which students may major in after twenty-seven hours of coursework above the 2200 level, including two literature courses and a linguistics course. A total of twenty-seven semester hours are needed for a Spanish major according to the General Bulletin of the university (1999–2000).

The course SPN 3201 is described in the General Bulletin of the university as follows: "Reading and Conversation (3 credit hours) SPN 2240 or equivalent. May be taken before or concurrently with 3310; not open to native speakers. This course focuses on reading and discussion of short literary works and/or cultural passages. In addition, the course also has a strong conversational component with emphasis on vocabulary building so that the student will be able to discuss certain topics in conversation" (1999–2000, 263).

The students enrolled in SPN 3201 have taken or have the equivalent of four semesters of Spanish from the following courses: SPN 1120, SPN 1121, SPN 1150, SPN 2200, and SPN 2240. This is an undergraduate-level course and is necessary for students majoring in Spanish at the university.

The course that was investigated for this study (the actual course observed, recorded, and analyzed) was chosen because of the following factors: availability and willingness of the instructor to participate in the study; meeting time of the course did not conflict with the researcher's other responsibilities; and content of the course reflected the area that was to be studied by the pilot study (i.e., authentic text and literature).

## TREATMENT AND ANALYSIS

In studies analyzing discourse, an important aspect of the methodology focuses on specific topics that are transcribed and analyzed (Lyons 1977; Keenan and Schieffelin 1976; Bransford 1976). In order to focus the analysis of this study (and following the methodology from the previously men-

**Figure 8.1**
**Situating Text-Centered Talk in Classroom Talk**

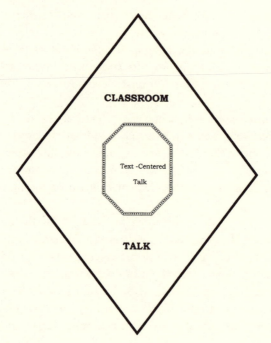

tioned studies), the classroom talk that will be transcribed and analyzed will be TCT; that is, classroom talk that is explicitly about the text being read and studied.

The talk recorded in the FLC was reduced, transcribed, and analyzed according to the levels of classroom talk previously defined: utterance, dialogue, discourse, and progressive discourse. Moreover, the methodology allowed the researcher to investigate the role of opportunities (or lack thereof) provided by the instructor(s) or student(s) in the development of classroom talk.

The following figures illustrate the focus and the first general process of analysis of this study. Figure 8.1 illustrates the focus of this study at a global level. Figure 8.2 illustrates the focus of this study at a microlevel, and the first step in analyzing the discourse.

Figure 8.1 outlines the initial framework of analysis. Although the diagram may seem inflexible, it was used to assist in focusing the analysis. The recorded data will not be randomly assigned to the corresponding sections. Figure 8.2 will assist in the holistic mapping of the classroom talk at a

**Figure 8.2**
**First Analysis of Text-Centered Talk**

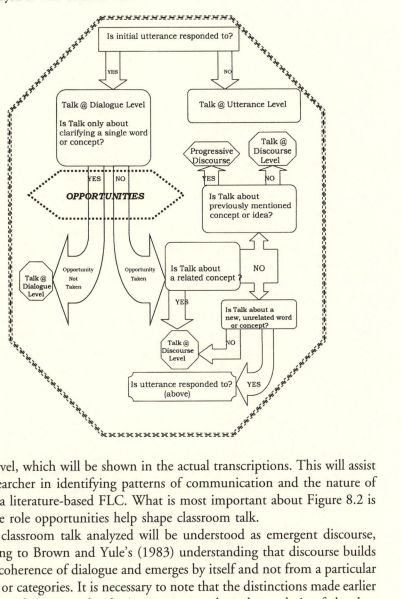

microlevel, which will be shown in the actual transcriptions. This will assist the researcher in identifying patterns of communication and the nature of talk in a literature-based FLC. What is most important about Figure 8.2 is how the role opportunities help shape classroom talk.

The classroom talk analyzed will be understood as emergent discourse, according to Brown and Yule's (1983) understanding that discourse builds on the coherence of dialogue and emerges by itself and not from a particular outline or categories. It is necessary to note that the distinctions made earlier between coherence and cohesion were central to the analysis of the data because coherence is responsible for the development of communication (Schiffrin 1994). This is not to say that cohesion (which is syntactically based as opposed to conceptually based) does not enter into building discourse, but within a sociocultural framework, coherence is understood as the driving force behind the emergence of discourse.

## THE FTCB

Discourse is one way that intellectual functioning is exhibited in college-level classrooms (Givens 1976). In order to understand better the cognitive aspects of classroom discourse, the FTCB (Givens 1976) was applied to the data. The FTCB is based on the work of Bloom (1956). As Givens writes: "The taxonomy is sequentially arranged from the knowledge level to the evaluation level. The 'higher cognitive processes' and 'higher levels of thinking' (referred to) are the higher levels on the taxonomy chart and are presumed to involve more complex or abstract thought processes than the lower levels" (1976, 13).

The FTCB assisted in analyzing the data at a cognitive level by analyzing utterance, dialogue, discourse, or progressive discourse that occurred during classroom talk. The FTCB objectively marked the overall and most common cognitive level (according to the FTCB) of the classroom talk in the literature-based FLC.

According to Webb, "the teacher's basic purpose is to guide students in the acquisition of knowledge and the development of intellectual skills" (1970, 50). The FTCB can determine if, as Givens states, "the central focus of the (classroom talk) is the acquisition of information or the utilization of cognitive processes in dealing with knowledge" (1976, 50). Logically, the more the students and the teacher "deal with knowledge" and utilize higher cognitive processes as described by the FTCB, the more discourse should be evident in the class as defined by this study. The FTCB also helped to further define the opportunities provided (if any) to enter into extended classroom talk. An additional benefit of using this instrument was determining the level of cognitive behavior in a literature-based FLC that should be reflected in the type of classroom talk recorded and analyzed.

There are seven increasingly complex levels of cognitive behavior, according to Givens (1976), and there are fifty-five sublevels that fall under the main levels, however, they are not arranged hierarchically. In keeping with the initial thoughts of Bloom (1956), the seven main levels of the FTCB (see Appendix) are:

1. Knowledge
2. Translation

3. Interpretation
4. Application
5. Analysis
6. Synthesis
7. Evaluation

The knowledge level makes up for about one-third of the total items on the FTCB, which has been subdivided into three categories:

1. Knowledge of specifics
2. Knowledge of processes to deal with specifics
3. Knowledge of universals and abstractions

These cognitive behaviors are all "memory level." That is, the individual does not have to take into account new information to take part in classroom communication.

The second level, translation, is self-explanatory when one looks at the FTCB. However, we should realize that this section may entail cognitive behavior expressed in either language. Understanding that this is a FLC, the classroom talk was not treated as pure "translation" in terms of cognitive behavior.

At the third level, interpretation, the individual understands how ideas are interrelated in the classroom. In the following levels (4–7), a person must use the knowledge he or she has or recently been exposed to. At the fourth level, application, a person must know the information well enough to be able to use it in a new situation. The fifth level, analysis, emphasizes the relationship and the organization of the elements of communication/discourse. During the sixth level, synthesis, a pattern of communication emerges that is unique to the situation and participants. At the last level, evaluation, the participants consciously judge and evaluate the information presented.

According to Webb, the FTCB makes the critical assumption, based on Bloom's *Taxonomy* (1956), that just because "intellectual abilities [cognition] become increasingly complex in nature [naturally] does not suggest that the higher levels are only present in the cognitive behavior of mature individuals, but rather, they can occur at each developmental stage, although in a different form" (1970, 52). Thus, cognitive development involves both the acquisition of knowledge and its utilization (Givens 1976).

Each instance labeled as utterance, dialogue, or discourse after the first step in analysis was complete was labeled as an exchange. The student utterances within the exchanges were then assigned a level from the FTCB according to the elements of communication and cognitive functioning present. The responses were then divided in order to separate the classroom talk into the cognitive levels of functioning set forth in the FTCB.

The FTCB reflects the cognitive level of student responses (tool use) and their roles in the development of higher mental functions (Vygotsky 1978) that are evident in Bloom's *Taxonomy* (1956). Also, the role of opportunities afforded by the instructor through classroom dialogue and discourse to extend communication into the higher cognitive levels was studied using the framework provided by Vygotsky (1978), Bloom (1956), and the FTCB.

## TEACHER INTERVIEWS

Three teacher interviews were conducted during the data collection processes. These interviews served the purpose of clarifying and defining the teacher's purpose and goals for the course. These data were used to understand further the role of the dichotomy of interpretation and expectation that has been defined in the previous chapter. These interviews will prove helpful in defining what teachers consider to be effective classroom talk in a literature-based FLC. Their responses will not, however, change the initial framework of the study. Questions or topics of discussion to be included in the interviews will address local (classroom) topics as well as curricular or global issues (Wells 1996; Woods 1986) encountered during the course of data collection.

## DATA COLLECTION

To answer the research questions, this study will follow the following guidelines for data collection:

• Classroom talk was recorded from various "whole units" of instruction. "Whole units" refers to complete instruction of the piece of literature being studied from its introduction to completion according to the syllabi provided by the instructor.

• Each whole unit was reduced, transcribed, and coded according to the level of classroom talk: utterance, dialogue, and discourse. Examples will be included in the later chapters of the study.

• The student responses during TCT were coded and analyzed using the FTCB.

• Teacher interviews were recorded, but not transcribed completely. Relevant segments of the interviews will be reduced and transcribed in the following chapters as needed.

## METHOD OF TRANSCRIPTION

The recorded classroom talk was reduced and transcribed, and the following symbols were used throughout the data to assist the reader and the researcher in further analysis. What follows are transcription conventions developed and used in conversation analysis by Brown and Yule (1981), further clarified by the use of examples (Johnson 1995).

/ indicates that the next speaker overlaps at this point:

    A: but they are at / school

    B: / aren't they at school?

// indicates that two speakers start simultaneously:

    A: // but they are at school

    B: // aren't they at school?

An asterisk (*) shows the point where the overlap ends:

    A: but they are at / school

    B: / aren't they at school?*

    A: I think so.

= indicates "latching," where there is no gap between utterances:

    A: but they are at school

    B: why are they at school?

+ indicates a pause

++ indicates a longer pause

In the event that a pause between utterances is five or more seconds, that time will be noted in parentheses after the symbol +++

    A: but they are at school?

    B: no +++ (6 seconds) they are at home, or

    A: but they are at + school?

    B: no ++ they are at home.

Single parentheses will be used when the researcher is not sure of the accuracy. Double parentheses will be used to indicate nonverbal sounds.

A: they are at school

B: (( cough )) no they are at home.

## SUMMARY

After reducing and transcribing, the data collected was analyzed using:

• Holistic mapping using the concepts, opportunities, utterance, dialogue, discourse, and progressive discourse (as previously defined) to guide the analysis of classroom talk. This is generally outlined in Figure 2.1.

• Givens's (1976) FTCB.

The transcribed data was then given to an outside observer to establish interrater reliability and trustworthiness after the observer was trained using the definitions of utterance, dialogue, and discourse and examples of each.

The outline provided assisted in understanding the emergent qualities of classroom talk, the role of opportunities (taken or not taken), and their affects on classroom talk in a literature-based FLC. The FTCB allows for the data to be analyzed according to its cognitive functions. By cross-referencing the analysis, a more precise and clearer picture of classroom talk and communication in a literature-based FLC occurred.

An underpinning of the sociocultural framework is the attention paid to cognition and the mind as a product of individuals interacting and communicating. The methods of analysis mentioned earlier, although linguistically driven, are cognitively focused. By cross-referencing and comparing data analysis, what emerges is a clearer picture of classroom talk and communication at a cognitive level through a sociocultural lens.

# CHAPTER 9

∞

# *The Reasons They Speak*

The present chapter applies the methodology for discourse analysis in a literature-based FLC. This data analysis offers insight into the later findings and further defines the inner workings of the methods used during the present study. The application of the methodology can be seen throughout this chapter in the selected examples of classroom talk.

The classroom talk was audiotaped, reduced, transcribed, and then analyzed according to the levels of classroom talk: utterance, dialogue, and discourse. The data were also analyzed using the FTCB.

The classes that were observed, recorded, and transcribed were all SPN 3201. This is the "bridge course" between language or linguistically focused courses and the purely literature-based courses such as "The Latin-American Short Story" or "Eighteenth-Century Spanish Drama." The catalogue from the university describes the course SPN 3201 as having a strong conversational component. This analysis sets out to understand what is meant by "conversation" (classroom talk) in a literature-based FLC such as SPN 3201.

The class was observed for a total of nine full weeks of class time. Also, the class was observed two more times later in the semester. The only difference noted in the two classes that were observed later in the semester was that the students had group presentations prepared about various cultural topics. The university in which the class is taught is on the semester system. A total of seventeen classes were observed during the nine weeks of instruction. There were no students who were native speakers of Spanish, although there were several that did have Hispanic heritage. In addition to the instructor, a total of twenty-one students gave the researcher permission to record, transcribe, and analyze their classroom talk: six males and fifteen females.

The instructor has been teaching Spanish for eighteen years and has taught this course three times before the present semester. The instructor is a native speaker of Spanish and holds a doctorate in Hispanic literature.

The seating arrangement for the class was traditional: five rows of four to six desks facing the front of the class. The instructor stayed in front of the class for the majority of the lessons observed and sometimes walked among the students while they were involved in group work.

## CLASSROOM ACTIVITY OUTLINE

Figure 9.1 is an outline of the general activities that took place in this particular class. The chart was constructed by the observer after listening to the data recorded, reviewing classroom observation notes, and interviewing three of the students as to the types and length of the activities or segments in the SPN 3201 class. Each student interviewed constructed the procedural elements and then agreed on the basic activities (general announcements and classroom duties, vocabulary and prereading, TCT, group work, grammar practice, and closing reminders) and the order in which they took place after they were interviewed. The only difference in the students' comments was about the amount of time spent in each activity (about a five-minute difference). Complete classes lasted from a minimum of 60 minutes to a maximum of 115 minutes. Activities surrounded by a dotted line took place during more than 50 percent of the classes observed. Activities surrounded by a solid line took place in more than 90 percent of the classes observed.

Some observed examples of general announcements and classroom duties performed by the instructor were greeting students, taking roll, asking if every student had a textbook, and handing out graded papers and tests. This generally lasted five minutes.

For vocabulary and prereading activities, each reading assignment in the text being used had a vocabulary section before the reading. The instructor would review the words in this section before beginning the classroom talk that surrounded the reading. This generally lasted ten to fifteen minutes.

For TCT, classroom talk centered on the authentic text and literature readings used in the class. This generally lasted fifteen to twenty minutes.

Group work centered around textbook activities in which students formed groups of two to four and answered questions related to the vocabulary, grammar, and theme of the unit being presented (e.g., immigrants

**Figure 9.1**
**Classroom Activity Outline**

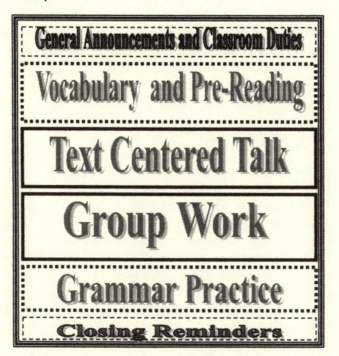

General Announcements and Classroom Duties

Vocabulary and Pre-Reading

Text Centered Talk

Group Work

Grammar Practice

Closing Reminders

in the United States). During this time, the students observed spoke in Spanish for the first few minutes then generally broke into English. The instructor would walk around the classroom answering questions and making sure that everyone was speaking Spanish, but the groups would begin to speak English as soon as the instructor walked away. The activities completed during the group work section of class were rarely discussed by the instructor and the class as a whole for evaluative purposes after the students had moved out of their groups. This activity generally lasted between twenty to twenty-five minutes.

During grammar practice, the instructor focused on a particular aspect of Spanish grammar by referring to activities in the textbook (for example, the conditional tense, the future tense, and the use of the subjunctive mood). This generally lasted five to ten minutes.

Some observed examples of closing reminders by the instructor were giving the date of next test, assigning homework, and setting due dates for papers. This generally lasted five minutes.

The instructor and the students spoke mainly in Spanish, and only broke into English when defining a new word or concept or giving an example of a grammar point. In groups, the students would begin in Spanish, but would revert to English when there was a disagreement or misunderstanding of the question. After completing the assigned tasks, the students would then speak in English until the next activity was initiated by the instructor. According to the classes observed for this study, classroom talk was teacher centered during all of the activities except for the group work.

## GENERAL LEVELS OF TCT

Figure 9.2 illustrates the percentage levels of classroom talk during TCT according to the classes observed. There were a total of eighty-four exchanges between the instructor and the students that varied in length. Of these exchanges, 18.86 percent were assigned to discourse, the highest level of classroom talk, and 74.44 percent were assigned the dialogue level of classroom talk. There were no instances of utterance-level talk observed, but the instances of teacher monologue (TM) were 6.7 percent.

Figure 9.2 represents the levels of TCT. In order to interpret such a figure, we need to inject a few concepts and questions into the framework. The first concept that must be appropriately placed is that of purpose. We should ask ourselves the purpose of the dialogues observed and analyzed. From my analysis, the purpose of the dialogues was not cognitive, but linguistic in nature. Dialogues, in this framework, are not the traditional form of interaction in which the teacher or students "act out" a particular script. Here, dialogues were used to talk about discrete point topics that extended into discourse only about 19 percent of the time in the classes observed. Now I turn to the purposes of discourse. The purposes here are not very clear, and discourse seemed to be more of a by-product of dialogue than a goal. The purpose of classroom talk, as seen earlier, was to establish an overall teacher-controlled dialogue. In some instances, the teacher's purpose was not very clear. That is to say, within the TMs, the talk that occurred did not have any particular bearing on the topics that were discussed. Again, we must realize that not everything that we do in a classroom has to have a particular purpose. But if only a small part of classroom talk is discourse, and perhaps awkward at that, then our words as instructors are at a premium. And these words must be carefully chosen if we are not allowing for student-to-student interaction or student-initiated talk in our classes.

**Figure 9.2**
**Distribution of the Levels of Text-Centered Classroom Talk**

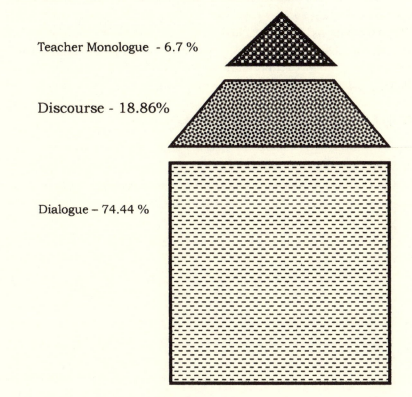

Teacher Monologue  - 6.7 %

Discourse - 18.86%

Dialogue – 74.44 %

## THE NATURE OF CLASSROOM TALK

The nature of classroom talk in the fourth semester, literature-based FLC observed was overwhelmingly at the dialogue level. As noted in Figure 9.2, 74.44 percent of TCT was dialogue. Within the level of dialogue there are several types exchanges. The following are examples of these exchanges.

Dialogue Example #1 is from an activity from the textbook that came after the assigned reading and is labeled as "¿Entendido?" (Understood?) in the textbook. In these sections, the students were asked to evaluate statements as "cierto o falso" (true or false) and to correct the false statements. The instructor always used this activity after the students read the passage for homework. This activity was generally preceded by a prereading or vocabulary activity that was labeled "Palabra por Palabra" (Word for Word) and "Mejor Dicho" (Clearly Stated). In the following example, a clear teacher-centered IRE pattern of communication is seen. The students have just read a selection about stereotypes.

The transcript has been separated further to show the amount of teacher talk versus student talk during this type of classroom communication. There were a total of nine "cierto o falso" questions that the instructor reviewed following the pattern below, but only the first three are shown as examples.

**Dialogue Example #1: Initiation-Response-Evaluation**

1. T: Vamos a hacer rápidamente en la página 128 el Cierto y Falso. Va-
2. mos a hacerlos muy rápidamente.
3. Los norteamericanos no saben gozar de los placeres de la inactividad.
4. ¿Cierto o Falso? +
5. Ss: Cierto.
6. T: OK. ¿Qué dice la lectura de los norteamericanos?
7. ¿Cómo se puede explicar eso?
8. ¿Cuál es, Cuál es según el autor el gran problema de los norteamericanos? +
9. Ss: Trabajan mucho. +
10. T: OK. Trabajan mucho, muy bien.
11. ¿Aquí qué pasa?
12. El ocio . . . ellos siempre tienen que hacer algo. Siempre quieren estar activos.
13. OK. Número dos: La televisión contribuye a formar y solidificar los
14. estereotipos. ¿Cierto o Falso? +
15. Ss: Cierto +
16. T: Los estereotipos son siempre ofensivos y se deben evitar. ¿Cierto o Falso? +
17. Ss: Cierto
18. T: Cierto.
19. Vamos a hablar de eso un momento.
20. ¿Por qué son malos esos estereotipos? Son divertidos, ¿no?
21. Pueden ser un cuento de chistes, no, para divertirse.
22. ¿Pero qué pasa con los estereotipos? +
23. S1: ¿Algunas personas creen que son verdad por todos? /
24. T: / Sí. ¿Qué pasa?

25. Que son falsos, o sea que el grupo es tan diverso.
26. Es como los Estados Unidos. Hay gente que le gusta trabajar mucho pero
27. hay gente que no le gusta trabajar. O sea, hay de todo. O sea, lo mismo
28. sucede en America Latina, en España. Es bien difícil decir a todos
29. los mejicanos les gustan las fiestas.
30. OK. La pregunta número cuatro.


If we take a closer look at this example, we will notice something even more interesting: The instructor has background setting patterns within the answers or explanations to the questions as in lines 10–12 and 16–21. In lines 19–21, the pattern is realized when the instructor answers her own questions. Again, lines 22–29 exemplify the classic IRE pattern of classroom talk. But in lines 24–29 we see another example of a background setting pattern. This pattern of talk was the primary method that the instructor used to determine if the students had read and comprehended the selected reading.

Dialogue-level classroom talk was also evident when the teacher began to ask questions about the topic of the reading as in Dialogue Example #2. In this example, the students had read a selection about music and were in the beginning moments of talking about the reading. The whole talk that revolved around this reading was at the dialogue level exemplified here.


**Dialogue Example #2: Un poquito de Música**

1. T: Vamos a hablar un poquito de la música. A repasar un poco.
2. ¿Qué canciones hispanas conocen ustedes muy bien?
3. ¿Qué son muy populares. Sean españolas, latinoamericanas, en la Amer-
4. ica Latina. (S1)? +
5. S1: Hmmm, ¿Ricky Martin? +
6. T: Sí, pero, ¿qué canciones de Ricky Martin? ++
7. S1: Uhmmmm +++ ( 7 seconds)
8. T: ¿El tiene alguna canción en Español?
9. S1: María
10. T: María. ¿Te gusta la canción de Ricky Martin? ¿Por qué?
11. S1: El ritmo es rápido.
12. T: El ritmo es rápido, muy bien. ¿De que trata la conción?
13. ¿De que es la canción? ++
14. S1: De una chica.

*Topic Shift*

15. T: OK. Otra canción popular, (S2). +++ (6 seconds)
16. S2: Chiqui, Chiqui, Boom, Boom.
17. T: OK. Yo no podría decir ese título.
18. ¿De que es esa canción? +
19. S2: De un amor por un hombre.
20. Es de lo que el hace sin ella con su corazón partida.
21. T: De un corazón partido.
22. ¿Y por qué te gusta la canción? +
23. S2: Tiene un ritmo muy rápido para bailar.
24. T: ¿Te gusta bailar?

*Topic Shift*

25. ¿Otra canción hispana que le gusta? (S3)?
26. S3: La bamba
27. T: La bamba, ¿te gusta? +
28. S3: Está bien. /
29. T: / Una canción hispana . . . buenísima, ¿no?


In this example, the talk did not later extend into the discourse level. This type of dialogue was typical when the readings focused on global or cultural topics and not specific stories or narratives as in Dialogue Example #3.

Dialogue Example #3 takes place after the students had read a story about a Cuban immigrant's experiences when beginning a new life in the United States. This example is typical of the TCT that took place when talking about the readings. It follows the IRE pattern as well, and more importantly, as will be shown later, it creates opportunities for discourse that are not taken by the instructor.

Dialogue Example #3 took place before the instructor led the class into the "Entendido" section as shown in Dialogue Example #1.


**Dialogue Example #3: Un Exiliado Cubano**

1. T: OK. La lectura que nosotros tenemos para hoy es sobre . . . es de una
2. situación de un exiliado cubano. Vamos a ver. ++

3. ¿Quién es el autor de la lectura? ¿Alguién sabe? Quién es el autor? ¿Que hace

4. el autor?

5. Luis Fernández Caudi. Es periodista en Miami.

6. Y como ustedes saben hay varios periódicos en Miami, varios periódicos

7. en Español.

8. Ahora lo que es bien interesante es que es un relato autobiográfico, de

9. su propia vida.

10. ¿De que trata la lectura, de que trata? ¿Qué hace este personaje principal? +

11. S1: El obtiene un trabajo con / Coca-Cola.

12. T: / El obtiene un trabajo en la compañía Coca-Cola. OK.

*Topic Shift*

13. ¿En que momento se desaroya, en que tiempo se desaroya el relato?

14. ¿Cuando, que año, a que año se refiere la historia, (S2)?

15. ¿No sabes?

16. ¿(S3), a que año se refiere la historia?

17. S3: Un mil noventa y . . .

18. T: Mil, Mil +

19. S3: / Nove..

20. T: / Novecientos ++

21. S3: ¿sesenta y uno?

22. T: Muy bien. Mil novecientos sesenta y uno.

*Topic Shift*

23. Entonces, hace cuántos años de esa fecha fue la revolución cubana?

24. ¿Hace cuántos años de esa fecha? +

25. S4: ¿Dos / años?

26. T: / Dos años. ¿La revolución comenzó en mil novecientos, (S5)?

27. S5: cincuenta y nueve.

28. T: / Mil novecientos cincuenta y nueve. Bien, así que apenas hacia dos años.

29. O sea que él acababa de llegar a vela a Miami. OK.

*Topic Shift*

30. ¿Qué profesión tenía el protagonista en Cuba? +

31. S6: Era abogado. /

32. T: / El era abogado.

33. El era abogado, ¿y cómo era su vida en Cuba?

34. ¿Cómo era su vida?

35. ¿Cómo es la vida de un abogado? /

36. S6: / Comfortable +

37. T: La vida es cómoda. Muy bien.

*Topic Shift*

38. ¿Cómo viste?

39. Muy elegante, cuando la gente viste muy bien.

*Topic Shift*

40. Pero ahora hay un cambio.

41. ¿Por qué no puede ser abogado en la Florida?

42. ¿Alguien sabe?

43. ¿Conocen las reglas? (S7)? No? ++

44. S8: ¿Hay que tener licencia? /

45. T: / Sí, obviamente para ser abogado, ser médico, hay que tener licencia.

46. Hay que pasar los exámenes. El famoso Florida Bar.

*Topic Shift*

47. De hecho, esto es muy interesante porque muchos inmigrantes vuelven a la

48. escuela graduada, la escuela profesional, para sacar la licencia de la

49. profesión. ¿Pero qué pasó con este señor, con el protagonista?

50. No podía ser abogado.

51. Hay que tener permiso, una persona que, obviamente el no era ciudadano,

52. ¿hay que ser ciudadano para trabajar en los Estados Unidos?

53. (S9), ¿por qué?

*Topic Shift*

54. ¿Qué hay que tener? /

55. S9: / Visa para trabajar. /

56. T: / Hay que tener una visa para trabajar, exactamente.

57. No hay que ser ciudadano. OK.

58. Vamos a hacer rapidamente las preguntas de "entendido," rapidamente.

Clearly, the IRE sequence is seen in this example, and we also notice more examples of instructionally embedded IRE in lines 1–12 and 37–52 where embedded IRE patterns are evident in lines 3–9, 38–40, and 49–51.

This type of classroom talk mainly addresses known-answer type questions where specific facts from the text are used as a point of reference and evaluation of text comprehension for the instructor.

Of the classes observed and analyzed, there were no instances of utterance-level talk by the students. In other words, the instructor responded to everything that the students said, therefore creating dialogue. However, there were numerous instances of utterance-level talk by the instructor. That is to say that the students were not given the opportunity to respond to questions asked by the instructor. These instances differ from the background setting pattern of teacher talk described before since there is no response or answer to the questions posed as is seen in the following examples.

**Utterance-Level Talk Example #1:**

1. T: A menudo no nos damos cuenta de que pensamos en términos muy
2. estereotipados. +
3. S4: Falso. ++
4. T: ¿Sí? ¿Por qué?
5. Entienden la oración, ¿A menudo no nos damos cuenta de que pensamos
6. en términos muy estereotipados?
7. No nos damos cuenta de los estereotipados.
8. Yo creo que es cierto.
9. En mi caso yo tengo unos estereotipos y no me doy cuenta que son
10. estereotipos.

The utterance-level talk occurs in line 4. "¿Por que?" (Why?) is never answered by any student. This example occurred during the activity described earlier as "¿Entendido?" and follows the typical IRE pattern. The instructor moved on to the next statement after line 10.

The next example occurred after the students read the selection about music. Notice that the instructor's question "¿Te gusta bailar?" is not responded to by the student, therefore, leaving the level of talk for the teacher, in this instance, at the utterance level.

**Utterance-Level Talk Example #2:**

1. T: ¿De qué es esa canción? +
2. S2: De un amor por un hombre. Es de lo que él hace sin ella con su corazón
3. partida. /
4. T: / De un corazón partido.
5. ¿Y por qué te gusta la canción? +
6. S2: Tiene un ritmo muy rápido para bailar. /
7. T: / ¿Te gusta bailar?
8. ¿Otra canción hispana que le gusta? (S3)?
9. S3: La bamba

The utterance in line 7 is never answered by the student, but the dialogue continues with Student 3's response in line 9. The importance of missed opportunities such as these will be discussed later.

The last selection of utterance-level talk took place after the students read about "Tapas" (appetizers) in Spain. In this example, the instructor has asked three consecutive questions, but only the third "¿Por qué dices que son malas?" is responded to by the student.

**Utterance-Level Talk Example #3:**

1. T: ¿Que tapas encontramos en un bar, en una
2. taverna? +
3. S5: Malos. +
4. T: ¿Recuerdan la lectura? ¿Que pasa con los turistas?
5. ¿Por qué dices que son malas? ++
6. S5: Son muy viejos, y el marisco, arroz.

This is another example of the IRE pattern of talk encountered in the classroom. Even though the dialogue does continue, in line 4 there are two instances of utterances that were not responded to by the students. Possible reasons for this will be discussed in the following chapter.

The original framework of this study did not address what has been realized and defined through the observations, transcriptions, and analysis as TM. TMs are instances of talk that are spoken by the instructor that may be intended to clarify a certain point or give an explanation, but the information given is not made use of by the instructor to assist in the development of dialogue to discourse. TMs usually took place at the end of an IRE sequence as seen in the following example. Being topically related to the dialogue, the TMs were treated as part of the dialogue surrounding the answer or response by the student.

**TM Example #1:**

1. T: Hay un juego de palabras con la palabra "ingenuo." OK.
2. Es una palabra nueva para ustedes.
3. ¿Qué significa la palabra ingenio, (S13)?
4. S13: ¿Wit? +++ (6 seconds)

*Topic Shift*

5. T: OK. La palabra ingenio tiene doble significado.
6. ¿Cuáles son los productos importantes en Cuba?
7. ¿Los productos de exportación?
8. ¿Ron, tabaco y azúcar?
9. El azúcar es uno de los productos más viejos y el azúcar, y para poder
10. producir azúcar hace falta un ingenuo azucarero, sugarmill, hace falta
11. un ingenio azucarero.

*Topic Shift*

12. ¿Y a qué clase social pertenecían la mayoría de los exiliados cubanos de
13. los años 60?
14. ¿A qué clase social? ++
15. S20: Alta /
16. T: / A la clase social alta.

*Topic Shift*

17. Así que hay un chiste, no, porque todos hablan de los ingenios que
18. tenían en Cuba. Porque todos tenían algo. Tenían tierra . . . pero el era
    abogado.
19. El dice (reading) sucede que yo no había tenido otro ingenio en Cuba
20. que el muy poco que quiso Dios ponerme en la cabeza.

*Topic Shift*

21. Qué significa ingenio en esta segunda oración? (reading again) Sucede
22. que yo no había tenido otro ingenio en Cuba que el muy poco que
23. quiso Dios ponerme en la cabeza.
24. ¿Así que se refiere a . . . ?
25. A la inteligencia. A, en inglés, Wit. Así que no tenía el ingenuo de
26. azúcar pero si tenía el ingenio que le dio Dios.

*Topic Shift*

27. Ahora, la segunda, la tercera parte del relato es cuado él llega a la
28. casa, y está la hija.
29. ¿Cuántos años tiene la hija?
30. ¿Cuántos años tiene la hija? /
31. S20: / Cuatro
32. T: Tiene cuatro años. Muy bien.

Lines 1–5 in this example follow the typical IRE pattern of talk. In lines 6–11, we notice once again the instructionally embedded IRE previously defined, and lines 12–16 are a typical IRE pattern once again. Lines 16–26 are defined as TM because the information presented to the students did not assist in developing or extending the dialogue into discourse and was not referred to in later classroom talk. Also, the main point of this TM was to give an explanation of the word "ingenuo." According to the student response in line 13, this meaning is already understood. If one were to take away lines 16–26, the classroom talk that followed would probably not have changed. As we see, the instructor follows an IRE pattern of communication again in lines 27–32, which are not at all related to the understanding of the word "wit" in Spanish.

## BEYOND DIALOGUE AND INTO DISCOURSE

TCT extended into the discourse level 18.86 percent of the time in the classes observed. The following example of discourse took place after the instructor had introduced and defined, with help from the students, the idea of "estereotipo" (stereotype).

**Discourse Example #1:**

1. T: Vamos a volver a la cuestión de los estereotipos. Son ideas que sé
   tienen.
2. Ahora. ¿Qué tipos de ideas son?
3. ¿Son ideas profundas o son ideas / simples?
4. S3: / Simples

*Topic Shift*

5. T: ¿Por qué? Cuál es un estereotipo? +
6. S3: Las rubias son muy divertidas. +
7. T: OK. Muy bien. Eso es un estereotipo.

*Topic Shift*

8. ¿Cuál sería un prejuicio? ++

9. S3: No me gustan las rubias / porque . . .

10. T: / Es algo que crees de verdad.

11. Por ejemplo, las mujeres hispanas no pueden manejar.

12. OK. ¿Cuales son unos prejuicios en la universidad?

*Topic Shift*

13. S4: Los atléticos. /

14. T: / Los atletas. ¿Qué pasa con los atletas? +

15. S5: Bobos. /

16. T: / Son bobos. ¿Y eso es cierto?

17. ¿Por qué es un estereotipo? ¿Por qué es un estereotipo? ++

18. S6: Porque (athlete) tiene un "four point o." ++

19. T: Hay atletas muy inteligentes. OK.

20. OK, otro estereotipo aquí en (la universidad). O en una universidad. ++

*Topic Shift*

21. S7: Todos los estudiantes son borrachos.

22. T: Sí. Eso es cierto. Que los estudiantes son unos borrachones. No es

23. que están sino que son, eso es muy fuerte.

*Topic Shift*

24. Otro estereotipo, ¿con el dinero?

25. Qué los estudiantes no tienen dinero. Y algunos sí tienen. Tienen mejor

26. coche, mejor carro del que yo tengo.

*Topic Shift*

27. Vamos a pensar un poco en lo que define un estereotipo.

28. ¿Qué define un estereotipo?

29. La cultura. el grupo social, /

30. S8: / La historia.

31. T: OK vamos a pensar.

*Topic Shift*

32. ¿Cuáles son los objetos o los subjetos de estereotipos? ++

33. S9: ¿Extranjeros? +

34. T: Extranjeros, muy bien.

35. Algo que uno no conoce.

36. ¿Qué más? +

37. S10: Raza.

38. T: La raza. Tiene que ver con lo que uno es. +

39. S11: La religión. +

40. T: La religión. Muy bien. Religión, Raza. +

41. S12: Dinero. +

42. T: Muy bien, la clase social.

43. Las personas de lugares específicos.

We can see how the students take advantage of the idea of stereotypes by first talking about a real-life example in lines 5–26. Also, within these lines the students distinguish stereotypes from prejudices. This example ends with the instructor and students naming causes for stereotypes and prejudices as noted in lines 28–40. It is interesting to note that even though students give one- or two-word answers, the instructor extends them in order to pose more questions and opportunities for the classroom talk to develop into discourse as seen in lines 5, 11–12, 16–17, 20, 28, 32, and 36.

Another example of discourse also includes (lines 1–8) an example of TM. The TM only served to introduce the beginning of TCT and not to clarify the meaning of "refranes" (sayings). However, despite the TM the classroom talk does extend into discourse.

**Discourse Example #2:**

1. T: OK. Nosotros hoy vamos a hablar un poco de los refranes.

2. Los refranes son bien importantes en todas las culturas, ¿no?

3. Pero especialmente en español, creo, somos muy refraneros.

4. sea usamos mucho, mucho, los refranes. En Puerto Rico tenemos muchos

5. refranes. Muchos heredados de la cultural española.

6. Bueno ustedes saben que también en la cultura hispánica hay muchos

7. piropos. Esto es otra cosa que están por allí dentro de la misma familia

8. de los refranes. ¿Alguién me puede decir lo que es un refrán?

9. ¿Qué es un refrán, (S1)? +++ (8 seconds)

*Topic Shift*

10. S1: No leí /
11. T: / ¿No leíste?
12. OK. Alguién que haya leído. ++

*Topic Shift*

13. S2: ¿Sayings? +

*Topic Shift*

14. T: OK. En Español. +
15. S2: ¿En Español? /
16. T: / Si, es parte del vocabulario.
17. ¿Cómo pueden definir un refrán? Si. +
18. S3: Frases hechas que no cambian con el uso. ++
19. T: OK. Si. Formas de decir. Una expresión idomática.

*Topic Shift*

20. ¿Cuales son algunos refranes populares?
21. En los Estados Unidos, en el inglés hay mucho refrán. ¿Cuáles son
22. algunos refranes populares, ahora? ¿Expresiones populares?
23. Bueno, expresiones no son necesariamente refranes, ¿pero cuales son
24. unas expresiones populares?

*Topic Shift*

25. Una expresión que yo no entendería. Ustedes saben yo soy de otra
    cultura.
26. Mis expresiones son como "Qué chevere," cosas así.

*Topic Shift*

27. ¿Qué dicen ustedes hoy en día? +++ (7 seconds)
28. S4: Cool /
29. T: / ¿Qué cool? Vamos a ver. Tienen que usar unas expresiones. ¿No
    saben?
30. Cuales son unas expresiones que usan hoy en día.

*Topic Shift*

31. S5: ¿Quieres expresiones o "sayings"? ++
32. T: Expresiones o refranes. /
33. S6: / OK
34. T: ¿Cómo cual? +++ (10 seconds)

*Topic Shift*

35. S6: Absence makes the heart grow fonder? /
36. T: / What? +

37. S6: Absence makes the heart grow fonder. /
38. T: / ¿Qué significa eso en español?
39. ¿Cómo pueden traducir una expresión como esa? ++
40. S7: You can't.
41. T: / ¿Cómo, (S7)? ¿Cuál es la primera palabra? La ausencia . . . /
42. S8:/ ¿Hace el corazón más fuerte? +
43. T: O sea, con la ausencia uno se da cuenta de lo que tiene.
44. No sé si será eso exactamente, pero.

*Topic Shift*

45. Yo quiero que ustedes con la persona que esté al lado hagan uno y dos de
46. "Alto."


   In this example, the instructor asks the students for examples of "refranes" instead of providing more of her own. This helps the students extend their communication beyond the dialogue level. Interestingly, the discourse ends rather abruptly at a point when the students are just beginning to use Spanish in new ways for them as seen in lines 40–46. After reaching the discourse level of communication, the instructor does not offer any more opportunities to extend the discourse further in this instance.

   Discourse Example #3 is particularly interesting because it shows how the classroom talk changes once the instructor relates to the students' own experiences when trying to understand the reading. This reading was about the colorful festivals and ceremonies of Mexico. The author, Octavio Paz, wrote about the visual and cultural elements one encounters when traveling through Mexico. After talking about what a "fiesta" (party) entails in Mexico, the instructor then asked the students to begin talking about ceremonies, and the one that took place the day before on campus. This led the class into talking about the upcoming holidays.


**Discourse Example #3:**

1. T: ¿Ceremónia? Ayer tuvimos una ceremonia en (la universidad). ¿Qué
2. es una ceremonia, (S5)? ++
3. S5: Un grupo de personas que están en un lugar. /
4. T: / OK. Muy bien. O un grupo de personas que están en un lugar
5. para celebrar.
6. ¿Y es una celebración formal o informal? /
7. S5: / Formal. /

*Topic Shift*

8. T: / ¿Formal, no? ¿Qué celebrábamos ayer en (la universidad)? ++

9. S6: ¿El cumpleaños de la unversidad? +

10. T: Cuantos años? 150 años, fue increíble. Asistieron, me imagino.

*Topic Shift*

11. ¿Qué cosas vieron en la fiesta de ayer? ¿Qué cosas vieron en la ceremonia? +++ (8 seconds)

12. S7: Comida.

13. T: Había comida. Había baile, danza? No.

14. ¿Qué había de las cosas que vemos aquí, colores, danzas, fuegos artificios, trajes, frutos, dulces.

*Topic Shift*

15. ¿Qué había en esta ceremonia? +

16. S8: Años y años de trajes. /

17. T: / Ah, los trajes antiguos.

18. ¿Qué más había en la ceremonia? +

19. S9: Canciones. /

20. T: / Habían canciones, muy bien. Habían canciones. ¿Qué otra cosa había? +

21. S10: Fuegos / de . . .

22. T: / Si, fuegos de artificio. A mi me sorprendió que tuvieran fuegos de artificio.

23. ¿Qué más tuvimos ayer en la ceremonia de celebración? Tuvimos trajes

24. antiguos. Tuvimos fuegos artificiales. ++

*Topic Shift*

25. S11: En el nuevo año. +++ (6 seconds)

26. T: ¿Cómo? ++

27. S11: ¿Nuevo / año?

*Topic Shift*

28. T: / No, pero ayer, ayer, ayer.

29. Canciones, comida. No sé si habían dulces pero si había comida gratis, ¿no?

30. Eso es decir que en (la universidad) hacemos fiestas también, ¿no? Y los estudiantes como ustedes, también, muchas fiestas.

*Topic Shift*

31. ¿Y que hacen los estudiantes en las fiestas?

32. Vamos a ver. ¿Qué hacen en las fiestas? +

33. S12: Beben /

34. T: / Beben, otra palabra para beber. Beben mucho, ¿que hacen? /

35. Ss: / Emborracharse. +

36. T: Muy bien, se emborrachan. La palabra de vocabulario muy

37. importante. Se emborrachan.

38. ¿Cuál es la bebida favorita de los estudiantes? +

39. S13: La cerveza. /

40. T: / Cerveza. ¿Y toman cerveza mejicana? Muy popular. / Dos Equis.

41. S14: / Corona.

42. T: Corona, muy bien.

*Topic Shift*

43. ¿Qué fiestas hay en los Estados Unidos? ¿Que ustedes celebran?

44. En febrero no hay una celebración? +

45. S15: Madri Gras. ++

*Topic Shift*

46. T: No, en febrero. Estaba pensando en fiestas / grandes.

47. S16: / El día de San Valentín. +

48. T: ¿Otro nombre para el día? ++

49. S17: El día del amor.

50. T: Bueno, muy cerca. El día de los enamorados, el día de los enamorados.

51. ¿Y a quien le gusta el día de enamorados? ¿A todo el mundo, no?

*Topic Shift*

52. ¿Qué hacen ustedes el día de los enamorados? ¿Qué haces el día de los

53. enamorados? ¿Vas a dormir, no? ++

54. S18: Normalmente, yo trabajo. +

55. T: Ohhhh, eso es un día aburrido. ¿Alguien hace algo? ¿Nadie?

56. S13: Estar borracho. ++

57. T: ¿Bueno es que sois todos solteros en la clase o que? ++

58. S14: Me emborracho. +++ (8 seconds)

59. T: Qué aburrido. ¿Normalmente que hace una persona que está ena-
morada? ++

60. S15: Gastar dinero. /

61. T: / Como gastar dinero. +

62. S16: Dulces. /

63. T: / Regalar dulces, OK, que más? ++

64. S16: Va a la cena. /

65. T: / Uno va al restaurante a cenar con le novio, amigo, esposo, esposa.

*Topic Shift*

66. Ahora, ¿ustedes creen que hay fiestas revueltas en los Estados Unidos?

67. Vamos a usar esa comparación.

68. ¿Hay fiestas revueltas? ¿Son las fiestas en la universidad tan revueltas

69. como en la universidad en México? Revueltas (writes on board). Una
palabra que usa Octavio Paz.

*Topic Shift*

70. ¿Qué significa revueltas? ++

72. S17: ¿Fiestas? /

71. T: / Sí, fiestas muy locas. ¿Son las fiestas revueltas de (la universidad)? /

73. S17: / Sí. +

*Topic Shift*

74. T: Depende de la fraternidad, ¿no? Bueno, vamos a hacer en la página

75. 41, en grupos.

Once again, the discourse suddenly stops after an attempt is made to define "revueltas" in lines 66–76, and the students move into groups. It is very important to note that all of the classroom talk that extended into discourse took place when the authentic reading was more cultural in substance than academic. In other words, classroom talk was more likely to extend into discourse when students did not have to interpret the meaning of "literature" and relied on their own experiences and expertise to talk about a cultural topic. There were no instances of discourse that revolved around "literature" (e.g., short stories, poems, essays, and the like).

From these observations and analysis, it is clear that students felt more comfortable extending the classroom talk when they were the ones who were the experts, not the instructor. The instructor was able to provide opportunities for this to happen and did listen and extend the student's responses as in lines 58–65.

## STUDENT-INITIATED TALK

There was not any student-initiated talk that assisted in building or extending the discourse in the classes observed. This is not to say that the students did not take part in the classroom discourse. However, the students did not initiate discourse (e.g., ask questions, ask for clarification, or make a new interpretation). They only responded to questions or statements made by the instructor that assisted the development of discourse. This is not understood as student-initiated discourse, but rather as student-supported discourse as seen in the Discourse Examples 1–3. Students did not usually speak unless called on by the instructor. This pattern placed the responsibility of initiating discourse on the instructor, and the supporting role to the students.

Also, during the moments of TCT in the classes observed, the students did not speak to each other in Spanish or English. The instructor acted as a filter for the statements and answers that the students gave in class. If the instructor accepted the statement or answer, then she would try to extend it by asking another student to give his or her opinion or answer. The main patterns of initiated communication (where dialogue or discourse begins) were from teacher to student to teacher to a different student, or teacher to student to same student to teacher to different student as seen throughout Discourse Example #3.

There is no avoiding the implications that this finding has on what the students believe that the instructor believes to be valuable in this setting: Ideas are not generated by the students, and understanding does not happen within students, but it is given to them by the instructor. And if the students understand Spanish, they will understand the readings and the instructor. Freire (1972) would place this into his banking system framework, where students will later "withdraw" information to use.

Later in this text, an introductory model for discourse analysis for the classroom teacher is offered. Within the guidelines, particular attention should be paid to what students say and when they say it. This may seem an obvious statement, but when we are in the classroom we may believe students' talking is always beneficial to their development. Some may argue that it would not be beneficial if it always marks the end of their contribution to classroom talk instead of the beginning.

## THE ROLE OF THE READINGS

The readings in this course are treated as "having intrinsic meaning." This is seen in Table 9.1. The purpose of this table is to show the cognitive level of the students' spoken responses to the instructor's questions about the authentic readings or texts that were used during the classes observed. The overwhelming majority of student responses (almost 60 percent) were those that dealt with knowledge of specifics (e.g., main character, where the story takes place, author, true-or-false statements, and the like). The percentage of students' responses that were at the knowledge-of-specifics level were 59.65 percent, and within this category 42.98 percent of the student responses gave a specific fact that can be found in the text as in Knowledge of Specifics Example #1.

The following example is from a reading about the role of bars in the social life of Spain and other Spanish-speaking countries.

**Knowledge of Specifics Example #1:**

1. T: Vamos a pensar en . . . no vamos a pensar en la bebida. Hay todo
2. un aspecto social que se da en los bares. ++
3. S15: Se puede comer en los bares. /
4. T: / Exactamente. Uno sale del trabajo y uno tiene hambre. Va a los bares y come.
5. Vamos a pensar en la condición social. +
6. S16: Para enontrarse con los amigos. +
7. T: Sí. Encontrarse con los amigos. Muy bien. habíamos dicho antes,
8. para hacer nuevos amigos.
9. Y hay una cuestión que tiene que ver obviamente con el mundo de los
10. negocios y el mundo profesional.
11. ¿Para qué va la gente a los bares? ¿Señor? ++
12. S14: Para hablar de los negocios. +
13. T: Cerrar tratos. ¿Qué hacen los hombres de negocios en los Estados Unidos?
14. Van al campo de golf. Hay más negocios en el campo de golf que . . . bueno
15. hay muchos negocios. Y lo mismo sucede en los bares en España.
16. La próxima pregunta. ¿Unos van todas las mañanas a tomar un café en
17. donde? ¿En donde se toma el autor un café? +
18. S15: En los bares.

**Table 9.1**
**Student FTCB Analysis**

| Cognitive Level | Number of Responses | FTCB Description | % of Total Responses | | |
|---|---|---|---|---|---|
| | | Knowledge of Specifics | | | |
| 1 | 11 | Reads | 4.824561404 | | |
| 3 | 15 | Identifies something by name | 6.578947368 | | |
| 4 | 9 | Defines a meaning of a term | 3.947368421 | | |
| 5 | 98 | Gives a specific fact | 42.98245614 | | |
| 6 | 3 | Tells about an event | 1.315789474 | | |
| | | | | **% of Knowledge of Specifics** | 59.64912281 |
| | | Knowledge of Ways and Means of Dealing with Specifics | | | |
| 11 | 1 | Cites Trend | 0.438596491 | | |
| | | | | **% of Knowledge of Ways and Means** | 0.438596491 |
| | | Knowledge of Universals and Abstractions | | | |
| 14 | 3 | States generalized concept or idea | 1.315789474 | | |
| | | | | **% of Knowledge of Universals and Abstactions** | 1.315789474 |
| | | Translation | | | |
| 18 | 16 | Restates in own wordsor briefer terms | 7.01754386 | | |
| 19 | 4 | Gives concrete example of abstract idea | 1.754385965 | | |
| 20 | 1 | Verbalizes from graphic representation | 0.438596491 | | |
| 22 | 2 | Trans fig stmts to lit stmts or vice versa | 0.877192982 | | |
| 23 | 1 | Trans from lang to Eng or Vice Versa | 0.438596491 | | |
| | | | | **% of Translation** | 10.52631579 |
| | | Interpretation | | | |
| 24 | 17 | Gives reason (tells why) | 7.456140351 | | |
| 25 | 3 | Shows similarities, differences | 1.315789474 | | |
| 26 | 16 | Summarizes, concludes from obs of evidnce | 7.01754386 | | |
| 27 | 3 | Shows cause and effect relationship | 1.315789474 | | |
| | | | | **% of Interpretation** | 17.10526316 |
| | | Application | | | |
| 30 | 9 | Applies previous learning to new situation | 3.947368421 | | |
| 31 | 4 | Applies principle to new situation | 1.754385965 | | |
| | | | | **% of Application** | 5.701754386 |
| | | Analysis | | | |
| 37 | 1 | Points out unstated assumption | 0.438596491 | | |
| 42 | 2 | Detects error in thinking | 0.877192982 | | |
| 43 | 1 | Infers, prpse, pt of view, thghts, feelings | 0.438596491 | | |
| | | | | **% of Analysis** | 1.754385965 |
| | | Synthesis | | | |
| 47 | 1 | Produces a plan, proposes a set of options | 0.438596491 | | |
| | | | | **% of Synthesis** | 0.438596491 |
| | | Evaluation | | | |
| 54 | 3 | Evaluates something from evidence | 1.315789474 | | |
| 55 | 4 | Evaluated something from criteria | 1.754385965 | | |
| | | | | **% of Evaluation** | 3.070175439 |
| | Total Responses 228 | | | Sum of % | 100 |

The responses given by the students in lines 3, 6, 12, and 18 were all very specific answers that came from the text read from homework the night before. In their responses, more importantly, the students were not applying their own knowledge or previous knowledge, analyzing the reading for various points of view (e.g., the effect this custom has on the bar owner's livelihood), synthesizing the information given and talks about what might the "average day" be like for a Spaniard, or evaluating this social habit (does it affect family relations or are only men allowed to go to the bars and interact like the author).

The opportunities to build discourse from classroom talk as in Knowledge of Specifics Example #1 are always present where the text is only treated as having intrinsic meaning, and not used to assist in the development of language and cognitive skills. The cognitive level of classroom talk only reflects the text that was read, and instead of only being rooted in the readings, the classroom talk is enveloped by the text giving little room for students to speak.

In Knowledge of Specifics Example #2, the cognitive level of classroom talk peaks for a moment (line 5), and we can see that when the cognitive level of the students' responses rises, so does the opportunity for discourse to develop in the classroom. This example is taken from the classroom talk that surrounded the reading about a Cuban immigrant's new life in the United States.

**Knowledge of Specifics Example #2:**

1. T: En mil novecientos sesenta y uno hubo elecciones en Cuba. ¿(S16)? +
2. S16: ¿Cierto? ++
3. T: Ahhh! ++
4. S16: Falso. /
5. T: / Falso. ¿Por qué? (S17)? +
6. S17: Hay un dictador. /
7. T: / Exactamente.
8. Cuando la niña llegó a su casa su padre se alegró de verla. +
9. S19: Cierto. +
10. T: No. Cuando la niña llegó a la casa . . . ¿quién llego a la casa? +
11. S19: El padre. /
12. T: / El padre. Es lo opuesto. El padre llegó a la casa no la niña.
13. ¿A la niña no le gustó el color del uniforme del color de su papá, (S18)? +
14. S18: Cierto.

In the previous dialogue, all of the student responses are at cognitive level 5 except for the response in line 6. This response was coded as cognitive level 30 because the student had to apply previously learned information that is not found in the text in order to answer the question "why?" in line 5. The question that arises from this classroom talk is: Why mention that there was a dictator if the students are not going to try and extend that idea a bit further (e.g., life under a dictator, is there "dictatorship" in the United States, and will there always be a dictator in Cuba). The discourse resulting from topics such as these could have very well extended the classroom talk.

The role of the readings in this course limited the classroom talk to that of being mostly dialogue (74.44 percent) and about knowledge of specific facts from the authentic texts and readings (59.65 percent). Part of the classroom talk (18.86 percent) was at the discourse level and the students' answers were cognitively higher than interpretation (application, analysis, synthesis, and evaluation—10.96 percent) of the student responses.

## SUMMARY

The majority (74.44 percent) of text-centered classroom talk in the course observed is dialogue. TCT extended into discourse 18.86 percent of the time during the course observed. The instructor did offer opportunities for dialogue to extend into discourse. However, there was no student-initiated dialogue that extended into discourse. Discourse revolved around culturally based texts and readings and not "literary" interpretations. The readings in this course were treated as having intrinsic meaning. This had a direct effect on the level of talk in the classroom inasmuch as the classroom talk was mostly at the dialogue level. This is seen in Table 9.1 where the students' cognitive behavior centered around knowledge of specifics (59.65 percent).

## CHECKING OURSELVES

I used Lincoln and Guba's (1985) four areas of inquiry that are designed to establish the trustworthiness of a study. They address the concerns that focus on the reliability of the findings by focusing on questions for researchers:

• Truth value: How can one establish confidence in the truth of the findings of a particular inquiry for the subjects (respondents) with which and the context in which the inquiry was carried out?

- Applicability: How can one determine the extent to which the findings of a particular inquiry have applicability in other contexts or other subjects (respondents)?

- Consistency: How can one determine whether the findings of an inquiry would be repeated if the inquiry were replicated with the same or similar context?

- Neutrality: How can one establish the degree to which the findings of an inquiry are determined by subjects (respondents) and conditions of the inquiry, and not by the biases, motivations, or perspectives of the inquirer? (290)

In order to establish the interobserver trustworthiness and agreement needed for the present study (according to the guidelines set by Lincoln and Guba [1985]), this study made use of an external observer who was trained by the researcher prior to being permitted to view and analyze the data.

The observer was trained to analyze the data according to the three types of classroom talk defined earlier: utterance, dialogue, and discourse (including progressive discourse). The outside observer was also trained to analyze the data according to the FTCB. The interobserver agreement was computed using the formula from Lincoln and Guba:

$$\frac{\text{Number of Agreements}}{\text{Number of Agreements} + \text{Number of Disagreements}} \times 100$$

An agreement between observers occurs every time the element of analysis (type of classroom talk or FTCB) matches each other's analysis. The interobserver agreement was calculated for the type of classroom talk and the FTCB:

Level of classroom talk: Interobserver agreement for the level of classroom talk was computed at 93.33 percent

FTCB levels: Interobserver agreement for the FTCB levels was computed at 91.23 percent

In accordance with Lincoln and Guba's (1985) areas of trustworthiness and reliability (truth value, applicability, consistency, and neutrality), the levels of agreement demonstrate that every precaution was taken to train an outside observer, and that the analysis of data followed the guidelines and methodology set forth in earlier chapters of this study. Also, the data for this present study was analyzed and discussed by two trained observers before admitting the final findings into the study. The final average inter-observer agreement (including the level of classroom talk and FTCB levels) was 92.38 percent.

# CHAPTER 10

## Extending Our Rationale

This chapter places my current findings into a precarious position. It is always easy to suggest what should have been done or what could be done in the future in order to take advantage of the classroom setting. What follows is not meant to imply that the courses observed did not serve a purpose or affect the language learning of the students. However, it is necessary to take an objective stance when interpreting the data and findings. Some may believe that what follows may seem to be too critical. I, too, believe it to be critical. It is critical that the field of SLA and foreign language education take a close look at what is supposedly taking place in classrooms that claim to build or improve oral proficiency through the use of authentic materials and texts. Students and educators should begin to think about what is meant by "oral proficiency" in these courses. Is it to master the IRE pattern of communication or to learn how to extend and challenge ourselves linguistically, cognitively, and conceptually?

## COURSE AND CURRICULUM

SPN 3201 has been given the unofficial title of "Bridge Course." That is, within the current curriculum, this type of course is designed to assist students in moving from classes that are focused more on building linguistic proficiency (learning grammar and vocabulary within certain cultural contexts) to more advanced classes. Students are required and expected to interact and communicate more in class as well as read more advanced materials in the courses that follow SPN 3201. Examples and descriptions of two courses that follow SPN 3201 are presented in order to further understand the role of SPN 3201 in the university's curriculum. Having successfully completed (i.e., passing with a *C* or better), the students may enroll in any of the following courses, which are taught completely in Spanish.

### SPN 4201: Masterpieces of Modern Spanish Literature

Reading and discussion of complete short works by Spain's most famous nineteenth and twentieth-century writers: El Duque de Rivas, Espronceda, Becquer, Alarcon, Blasco Ibanez, Unamuno, Aleixandre, Lorca, Machado, Matute, Arrabal, Cela.

Evaluation: There will be four or five 1 to 2 page take home essays, three hour exams, and no final exam (prerequisites: SPN 3100 and SPN 3101 or equivalent).

### SPN 4520: Spanish-American Culture and Civilization

The purpose of this course is to help students gain a clear understanding of the Latin American heritage and cultural milieu. The selected materials deal with past and current attitudes and perceptions prevalent in some parts of Latin America. In order for students to really understand, appreciate, and possibly identify with the dilemmas posed in the literature, it is necessary for them to acquire an understanding of the dynamics of how and why Latin American society and culture actually functions in different situations. In order to reach this goal, the students will read, view and write about the documentary "El espejo enterado," will read literary texts, and will view films dealing with, but not limited to the following cultural issues: Native cultures of America and the Spanish conquest, immigration, political structure, and gender cultural expectations. Existing customs, as well as myths, will also be explored in terms of their affects on socialization and acculturation.

Class Participation: 30% Students are expected to read and participate in class. Frequent and thoughtful participation is evaluated in class and online. Attendance and punctuality are very important, and any more than one (excused or unexcused) absence will hurt your final grade.

If we take a close look at these two course descriptions, the students who enroll in them after SPN 3201 will be expected to "read, view and write about the documentary 'El espejo enterado,' will read literary texts, and will view films dealing with, but not limited to the following cultural issues: Native cultures of America and the Spanish conquest, immigration, political structure, and gender cultural expectations. Existing customs, as well as myths, will also be explored in terms of their affects on socialization and acculturation" (from SPN 4520) as well as read and discuss "complete short works by Spain's most famous nineteenth and twentieth-century writers: El

Duque de Rivas, Espronceda, Becquer, Alarcon, Blasco Ibanez, Unamuno, Aleixandre, Lorca, Machado, Matute, Arrabal, Cela" (from SPN 4201). Given that the nature of the text-centered classroom talk in the SPN 3201 course observed was overwhelmingly dialogue (74.44 percent) and mostly based on knowledge of specifics (59.65 percent), it is reasonable to question how well the students will be able to participate and fulfill the course requirements or meet the goals of the SPN 4201 and SPN 4520 courses.

The cognitive functions needed to perform the tasks stated in the two course descriptions—application, analysis, synthesis, and evaluation—only took place 10.96 percent of the time during TCT. Obviously, there are many variables in these courses. However, if students in the courses that follow SPN 3201 are being graded and held responsible for performing high-level cognitive functions in Spanish, then at the very least they should have been afforded the opportunities to do so in the previous course, SPN 3201. But, as has been shown, the students rarely extended into the type of communication that ostensibly will be required of them in later courses.

To completely understand the place and role of SPN 3201, it is necessary to see how the students were prepared for SPN 3201. The introductory courses of SPN 1120, SPN 1121, SPN 1150, and SPN 2200 that precede SPN 3201 have as stated objectives within the curriculum: to build vocabulary and grammar knowledge, and basic conversation skills as well as cross-cultural awareness (General Bulletin of the university [1999–2000]).

The course description for SPN 2240 is:

Intermediate Spanish completes the intermediate Spanish skills sequence, and finishes the review of grammar skills sequence begun in SPN 2200. Students deepen their functional skills in comprehending, speaking, reading, and writing Spanish. And gain an overview of Hispanic cultures in various countries. May not be taken by native speakers. This course is a prerequisite to SPN 3201 and SPN 3101.

- Participation and Attendance: 25%
- Homework and Workbook: 20%
- Written Exams: 30%
- Oral Interviews (midterm): 10%
- Final Exam and Oral Interview: 20%

SPN 2240 has the objectives stated as: "In this course you will expand your knowledge of culture, history, and daily lives of Spanish-speaking peoples of the world. By the semester's end you will be able to carry on conversations beyond the ability to express simple physical or concrete needs. You will also learn to identify current and past contributions made by

Spanish-speaking peoples to world literature, art, music science and commerce. The course will include some review of grammar principles as they pertain to improving your ability to converse."

Interestingly, the students enrolled in SPN 2240 will by the semester's end "be able to carry on conversations beyond the ability to express simple physical or concrete needs." That is, the students will be able to interact and communicate beyond the level of knowledge of specifics. Although the students were able to communicate in Spanish above the level of knowledge of specifics (39.35 percent of the time), it is unclear if the students' oral proficiency made any real progress at all. SPN 2240 includes two oral interviews as part of the syllabus. Are these oral interviews given and graded in the same manner as the interviews in SPN 3201? If not, then how does one really know, how do students know, if the course goals and objectives that relate to oral proficiency and "deepening functional skills" have been met? This will be addressed later in this chapter.

The following is the course description from the course that was observed:

The main goal of this course is to build student's oral proficiency while increasing their awareness of Hispanic culture. Reading, writing, and listening skills are practiced extensively. The course is designed for the intermediate to advanced students to make them aware of the historical, political, social, artistic and literary developments in the Spanish speaking countries during the 20th century. Readings, writing assignments, films, and listening activities will provide a framework for interactive discussion sessions and classroom presentations.

Evaluation Performance: (from current course syllabus)

Tests include four exams, which focus on knowledge of the vocabulary, grammar, and culture studied in each unit. Speaking is evaluated through daily participation in class and during the oral exams. All exams include a written section, and two of them an oral presentation to be done with a classmate. Completion of the Cuaderno will be included in the final grade.

Grades: (from current course syllabus)

• Participation and Attendance 30%
• Homework and Workbook 30%
• Written Exams 20%
• Oral and Written Exams 20%

The main goal of the course, as stated earlier, is "to build student's oral proficiency." The current data analysis shows that the pattern of communication chosen by the instructor during TCT in order to reach this goal was teacher-centered, student-supported dialogue about specific facts. If we keep in mind the course description and objectives for SPN 2240, this goal (of generating concrete, specific dialogue) had already been addressed and, arguably, met. If this course was to "build oral proficiency" then can oral proficiency improve (beyond the goals set in SPN 2240) in the current classroom environment?

## ORAL PROFICIENCY

The present course had two oral exams built into the course's system of evaluation. They accounted for 20 percent of the student's grade according to the syllabus. In thinking about the answer to the question—can oral proficiency improve in the current classroom environment?—we must first try to understand the method for evaluating oral proficiency by the instructor in the course observed.

The researcher was allowed to observe and record five of the first oral exams (a total of one hour). All of the examinations followed this pattern (in Spanish):

Greetings

Talk about plans for the weekend or holidays

Questions and talk about the student's favorite reading

Discrete point questions about the student's favorite reading and other readings

Good-byes

Each oral exam took from ten minutes to the maximum of fifteen minutes. During the exam, the instructor did not take notes or make any marks on any forms. After the exam was over and the student had left the room, the instructor wrote the student's grade down by his or her name on the sign-up sheet for the oral exams. The method of grading was check minus, check, check plus. When asked how the instructor interpreted these marks, the instructor informed the researcher that check plus was an *A*, check was a *B*, and check minus was a *C*. The instructor also offered the comment that the main purpose of these oral exams was to build confidence in the student's ability to speak Spanish.

The researcher had an opportunity to observe students that were evaluated as check plus, check, and check minus. Interestingly, all of these students demonstrated that they could speak Spanish beyond the dialogue level of communication and that they could apply previous learning as well as synthesize and evaluate. The talk that took place during the oral exams did not mirror the talk that took place during the class. All of the students observed extended themselves much more into the discourse level of communication because they were given the opportunity. This type of talk happened while communicating about the student's favorite story. Interestingly, the instructor, during the classes observed, never asked the students which was their favorite story.

This observer has had four years of training and experience with oral proficiency exams in English as a Second Language, and many more years training in oral proficiency exams in foreign language education. According to this researcher's experiences, during the aforementioned years of evaluating the oral proficiency of L2 learners, it is difficult to understand how the use of such an undefined rubric truly evaluates a student's oral proficiency, and, therefore, the development (or "building") of oral proficiency throughout the semester. The use of this rubric places doubts on whether the students will be able to participate and communicate effectively in Spanish in more advanced courses because they have not been appropriately evaluated nor have they been given feedback about specific points on how to develop and improve their oral proficiency.

This is not to say that the instructor was not trained in oral proficiency interviews (OPIs) or not familiar with the American Council on the Teaching of Foreign Languages (ACTFL) guidelines. The instructor offered that she had been trained in the use of the OPI early in her professional career. But, as we see, that training was not applied to the oral exams for this course.

Also, an OPI- or ACTFL-focused curriculum is not being suggested. What is being suggested is that instructors use the academic tools at their disposal to assist them in evaluating students' progress through their courses. If students are not progressing linguistically, then questions and issues must be raised, especially if a course is designed with an oral proficiency focus or component. The linguistic needs of our students are varied, but we should have in place an instrument that all instructors are familiar with and use in order to properly serve them. This does not have to be difficult to put into place. We test students with entrance exams, and then (most of us) rely on the particular classes to evaluate their L2 linguistic proficiency, and each class may have a different instructor who holds some skills or abilities higher or more important than others. What may result is a lack of consistent feedback to our students, which may lead them astray in the future. Students may believe that after passing four courses of Spanish they are ready to handle and approach cognitively demanding situations in the L2 because they believe they have the linguistic skills. Here is where some of our students receive a rude awakening. In the classes observed, as stated, there were not any students that initiated talk in the classroom nor did they speak to each other in Spanish about their reactions (if any). If we translate this lack of cognitive initiative into a real-world setting, a person may become tired of having to ask the right questions in order to find out just what the student believes. As is well noted in our field, general intelligence and language acquisition are not interrelated unless there is a biological reason.

## "DISCRETE" FLCS

The role of the text in the course observed, as stated earlier, was one of having intrinsic meaning. That is, students answered discrete point questions about the texts rather than becoming involved in an extension of dialogue that may have resulted in discourse and other opportunities for them to speak in Spanish beyond the teacher-centered pattern of communication. Understandably, instructors do have to check for students' comprehension of assigned readings. However, comprehension check exercises, in and of themselves, should not constitute the majority of TCT if the main goal of the course is to increase the students' oral proficiency. These readings as mentioned before do not produce meaning (Lotman 1988). As noted before, the instructor did have the students work in small groups (two to four students), but did not take the opportunity to evaluate the students' in-group participation, therefore the in-group did not create opportunities for extension of class talk beyond the dialogue level.

During the classes observed, there was no evidence of social speech (Vygotsky 1978), nor of intersubjectivity (Wertsch 1998) as previously defined in this study. There also was not any evidence of coconstruction of information or meaning (Wells 1999) between the students or the between the students and the teacher. This is believed to be the case because the main goal of the course within the activity setting (Tharp and Gallimore 1988) that was guided by the instructor was restrictive as shown in the previous chapter.

## INSTRUCTIONAL CONSIDERATIONS

The instructor of the course observed succeeded in creating a comfortable classroom environment for the students. The instructor was well prepared with planned lessons and assignments for the students. She had a good rapport with the students, and those who were later interviewed in order to establish the classroom activity outline commented that the instructor was always very personable and well prepared for class.

During the course of the observations, the researcher and instructor often exchanged comments on how the class was developing and other issues that concerned foreign language education or SLA. The department in which the instructor teaches invited one of leading educators and researchers in SLA to speak to the faculty, graduate students, and the general university population. The instructor and I entered into a discussion about the purpose of bringing such a noted scholar to the university. The instructor then offered the comment that her field was that of literature and Hispanic studies, and that she was not familiar with the field of SLA or applied linguistics. Although a passing comment, this self-observation is very important inasmuch as the instructor's main concern for the SPN 3201 is the acquisition of a foreign language according to the goals and objectives of SPN 3201 stated earlier in this chapter.

The instructor has eighteen years of experience teaching foreign languages and literature and has taught SPN 3201 three times (including this time). It is obvious by watching her teach that she is very comfortable in front of a classroom and can manage the daily activities well. However, it is disconcerting that after teaching a foreign language, at one level or another, for eighteen years the instructor considers the fields of SLA and applied linguistics not her own. Understandably, after achieving a doctorate in Hispanic literature, one would tend to say that his or her area of study is Hispanic literature.

The instructor understood the value of reading in Spanish to be that reading helps increase vocabulary, grammar skills, and comprehension skills and assists students in the development of critical thinking that would then transfer into improved oral proficiency. Arguably, the underpinnings of the effects of reading in a foreign language, as stated by the instructor, are reasonable. However, in the course observed, there was very little evidence of critical thinking in the transcripts analyzed, much less the development of critical thinking skills. Logically, then, one can conclude from the supposition made by the instructor (that critical thinking assists in the development of oral proficiency) that there was very little, if any, development of oral proficiency due to the paucity of evidence of critical thinking by the students in the course observed.

The instructor also noted that challenging the abilities of students and the development of critical thinking skills is very important because the students will need them in later, more advanced courses in the department (as noted by the examples given earlier in this chapter). As noted earlier, it is difficult to see how a teacher-centered, student-supported dialogue about specific facts can be challenging and lead to critical thinking.

The instructor did say that in order to incorporate reading materials successfully in the classroom it is necessary to go beyond the text and engage the students in reflecting on their own experiences. To her credit, the instructor did try to incorporate this outlook into the course. But, for the reasons of time or activity type, she was not able to extend the classroom talk that was based on students' own experiences as much as one would have thought.

## TEXT AS TOOL

This investigation has presented language as the main tool by which we understand and shape the worlds in which we communicate (Halliday 1978). The research reviewed earlier has also alluded to "text" as encompassing all spoken and written language (Bakhtin 1984). However, the course observed, according to the findings of the data analysis, used the texts, rather than spoken language as the main tool that shaped the classroom environment. Using the text as a tool to guide classroom talk in hopes of building oral proficiency is reasonable. However, in the course observed the text used listed several communicative strategies that were to be brought about by the use of the readings as well as other classroom activities.

The following is a list of all of the communicative strategies incorporated into activities that surround readings that were observed during the present study. The instructor's manual of the class text states that the "Estratregias comunicativas" section is new to the second edition. It provides a list of expressions to help the flow of conversations. There are expressions for connecting, reacting, starting, continuing, and ending exchanges. The following list has been translated into English.

Inviting someone

Accepting or refusing an invitation

Asking for permission or forgiveness

Comparing and contrasting actions or things

Giving advice

Repeating what someone has said

Using and understanding body language

Learning how to finish a conversation

Getting someone's attention

Expressing nostalgia

After further review of the TCT, there were not any instances that the students used any of these communicative strategies. Furthermore, the instructor did not have the students try to use these communicative strategies, which may have led to further opportunities and classroom talk beyond the dialogue level.

The previous conclusions about communicative strategies further limit the use of the text and its potential to assist the students in obtaining the main objective of the observed course: to build student's oral proficiency. The communicative strategies, or any part of them, may have been useful during the oral proficiency exams as an informal checklist (at the very least) used by the instructor to evaluate the students' oral proficiency. But they were not used and were not apparent in the construction of the oral exam by the instructor given the types of questions asked during the oral exams observed.

The instructor mentions that this was the first time that this particular text was used in this course, and that she would use it in next semester's SPN 3201 course as well. She believes that a good textbook eases the planning of the class and provides engaging materials as well as prepares students for classroom discussions while reinforcing their grammar skills. Kramsch's views regarding the role of explanation and understanding of the text in the FLC are restated:

Explanation is more directed towards the analytic structure of the text, understanding is more directed towards the intentional unity of discourse. [That is to say] that the teacher can explain and teach the rhetorical structure, the form and content of the text, but an understanding of the values, intentions, and beliefs embedded in the text can only be achieved through open discussion and negotiation of meanings. According to Ricouer (1976) interpretation is a dialectic dynamic process by which the reader surpasses both explanation and understanding and "appropriates" the text for himself. (1985, 357)

In summary, the appropriation of the text happens when the students and the instructor are involved in a negotiation of discourse and ideas. The selection of an appropriate text for the students' linguistic level, rather than the language (linguistic tools) may be used to support higher or more complex cognitive skills throughout the classroom talk.

In closing, what may be one of the most important instructional implications from this study is that we are better able to understand what instructors believe to be is the actual purpose of using authentic texts and readings in the teaching of a foreign language. These beliefs, according to the instructor observed, are based on superficial readings for specific information in the hopes of building a vocabulary base that will assist in building oral proficiency. However, if one is to take this perspective, then we must also offer opportunities for the students to engage in the practice of education (Wells 1999).

Wells's (1999) guidelines are central to creating not only a productive learning environment, but they also form the foundation of the modern FLC where cognition and thinking are just as important, if not more so, than the language being used to build understanding, knowledge, and, in the long run, proficiency.

## FURTHER CONSIDERATIONS

I have been able to clarify many areas within this text, however, other areas of interest have been brought to light by the present data collection and analysis. These areas spring from the original framework of the study: sociocultural theory. Within sociocultural theory, learning takes place in the activity settings (Tharp and Gallimore 1988) of the classroom.

It is within this framework that the present FLC has been observed and the data analyzed, and through this, we are able to understand that when one speaks of a "discussion" in this class, he or she is most likely talking about a teacher-centered student-supported dialogue. Lave and Wegener state that from a sociocultural perspective learning is not to be measured in terms of the individual, but rather in terms of "increased participation in communities of practice" (1991, 49). As Forman (1995) notes, what matters most is that students be able to take part in discourse within a setting that builds a sense of community.

If we think about "meaningful practice" in a FLC based in authentic readings and texts, then what comes to mind is a classroom that evolves and revolves around the plans of the instructor. If these plans are to succeed in extending classroom talk beyond the dialogue level, then there must be opportunities for exploratory talk, coconstruction of meaning, and scaffolding as defined earlier in the study.

This type of meaningful practice would also include the students engaging in active mental participation and development of cognitive abilities in the L2. As Anton states, "cognitive development originates in social context" when teachers promote active mental participation (1999, 83). The data analysis has shown that the cognitive development promoted in this class was mostly that of answering specific questions, which mostly took place at the dialogue level of talk. Interestingly, the few instances of higher mental functions (Vygotsky 1978) took place at the level of discourse during classroom talk. The FTCB has reflected Bloom's (1956) beliefs that active mental participation in a social context may lead to the use of higher cognitive skills. It follows that classroom talk that extends itself into the level of discourse or exploratory talk (Wells 1999) may also promote the use of language and the development of more "linguistic tools" in order to promote and support higher cognitive functions and skills in the FLC.

The use of texts in the FLC is nothing new. But, if we are to truly engage the students in meaningful practice, then the norms of communication that envelope the TCT in a FLC such as SPN 3201 have to be reconsidered. The norms set out by the instructor ultimately affect the discourse practices of the classroom community (Forman 1995). The observed discourse practices in the present course are based much more on the coherence of classroom talk than on the cohesion of the same as defined previously. Classroom talk that is coherent is understandable inasmuch as the questions asked already have answers, and students have to understand the text in order to participate. Classroom talk that is cohesive uses the text to build discourse and communication around ideas that come from students and teachers understanding each other.

Finally, this study has brought to light a dichotomy that is defined as the stated versus the enacted curriculum (Smithson 1995; Tobin 1997). Obviously, the stated curriculum is what students are told the class is going to encompass and what they are expected to learn from the course. The enacted curriculum is the reality of the day-to-day unfolding of the patterns of interaction and norms of communication in the classroom environment. Hopefully, the stated and enacted goals and objectives of any given course are, within reason, identical. However, whenever we encounter two vastly different curricula, we must then begin to ask questions so that our purpose as educators does not become just words on paper, but instead, ideas and thoughts from our students. This dichotomy is affected by what I discussed as interpretation and expectation. It will not be an easy task taking students who are accustomed to a set pattern of expectations and communication in a classroom and placing them into another classroom that attempts to incorporate a new framework. The teachers and the students will need to have a shared understanding of what the goals of the course are: linguistically, cognitively, and by subject. Even though one goal should not give way to another, hopefully, they will work together to promote cognitive and linguistic growth while coming to terms with the material being presented.

## RECOMMENDATIONS FOR INSTRUCTION

The following recommendations were made after reviewing the findings from the data analysis. They are in no particular order of importance. Although these may be interpreted as specific recommendations for this particular course (SPN 3201), it is possible to extend the following suggestions further in other FLCs when approaching classroom discourse while using authentic texts or literature.

In order to move beyond an understanding of the cultural value of literature in a FLC (Barnes 2000; Kempf 1995; Davidheiser 1977; Steiner 1972), readings may be presented as part of an ongoing discourse of a classroom environment in which students reflect on their own values in relation to those presented in the readings. This approach may afford the students the opportunities for discourse that are based on personal observations about the readings and literature.

It is within this area that we can apply our notions of students acquiring diversity in being, and not just understanding. Students who reflect their own values and understanding throughout the readings may begin to view themselves, as well as the text, in a different light.

An awareness that discourse is a process and not only a product of classroom talk allows the instructor to move beyond the strategies for teaching authentic texts in a FLC (Katz 1996; Chamot 1994; Kumaravadivelu 1992; Santoni 1971). This perspective allows us to further understand the implications of the use of texts on the developing linguistic systems and communicative strategies of students. We know from our daily lives that we usually do not go up to any person and begin to talk to him or her at length without first becoming comfortable and having a purpose. Our classrooms are not any different. Discourse takes time to develop. But once that time has passed, it is crucial to move beyond simple exchanges. If not, we become bored with the "small talk" in our classrooms and tune out, because the answers are already known.

According to Frye (1984), the analysis of literature does not lead to an appropriation of meaning. It is when students interpret the literature that opportunities for discourse and appropriation are created in the FLC. This is not to say that literary analysis needs to be removed from the FLC. Just the opposite, by using literary analysis, students may be able to better interpret the text and appropriate it. This may include presentations, papers, group discussions, and forums. By no means am I suggesting that we re-move the literary aspects from L2 classrooms. What I propose is including a cognitive aspect in hopes of promoting the linguistic goals of the various courses and curriculums.

Instructors may want to ensure that the classroom talk not only conveys information that is to be learned (the text), but also provides opportunities for students to receive linguistic input and generate linguistic output in order to acquire a L2 (Fillmore 1982). Here, the instructor has to approach students' contributions with a "what if . . ." perspective: What if we talk more about this point, where will it lead us? What if I ask the student to explain further? What if other students want to give their views on the subject? By providing opportunities, many "what ifs" can be taken advan-tage of.

Social speech (Vygotsky 1978) in the FLC can be nurtured by the in-structor by providing opportunities to enter into discourse about a particular reading, and this, in turn, may lead to the linguistic as well as cognitive development of the students (Halliday 1993, 1978). Here, the underlying foundation of classroom discourse is a sense of community—not only the sense of a community of students, but as a community of readers that are exchanging ideas and coming to conclusions based on the text and their own interpretations. Todorov (1984) states that meaning implies commu-nity. In the FLC, instruction that reflects a sense of community in the classroom may allow for more development of linguistic and cognitive skills though an ongoing classroom discourse in the foreign language.

Instruction that focuses on discourse cohesion (context) may be more likely to produce opportunities for discourse than instruction that centers around the grammatical relationship between utterances (Coulthard 1977). Instruction that focuses on the understanding of language is also, in part, centered on the understanding of the speaker (Rommetveit 1979b). Instruc-tion in a text-based FLC that allows for the speaker to be understood (the meaning) through language being spoken may allow for students and the instructor to create more opportunities for intersubjectivity and negotiation of meaning.

## RECOMMENDATIONS FOR EVALUATION

This section offers some suggestions as to how instructors may approach the evaluation of classroom talk in a text-based FLC similar to the one studied. These recommendations are presented in no particular order of importance, but they are crucial inasmuch as they lay the foundation for linking the evaluative side of cognition and discourse in the L2 classroom.

- Use of the OPI to establish oral proficiency levels throughout the semester in order to better understand the linguistic development of students, and to provide concrete feedback to the students in courses such as these. This would include training instructors in the use of the OPI.
- Active teacher evaluation and preplanning of in-group activities in front of the whole class. Although time-consuming, these evaluations may provide opportunities for discourse in the classroom and provide the students with in-group opportunities for social speech and coconstruction of information.
- Synchronic and longitudinal evaluation of students by instructors using the same evaluation method (the OPI) may allow for more accurate reflection of the students' linguistic and cognitive skills over a period of time. Also, students who want to enter the foreign language teaching field will have a deeper understanding of their abilities and skills in the foreign language.

## IMPLICATIONS

This text has attempted to demystify sociocultural theory and discourse analysis. However, due to the very nature of academic inquiry, every topic for further research that presents itself after the initial framework and approach has been established cannot be dealt with due to the previously delineated boundaries. As such, further research in the area of discourse in literature-based FLCs is needed at all levels. Future analysis should concentrate on the interplay and relationship that courses within a curriculum have with each other to better understand the dynamics of assessment, instruction, materials, and language with the classroom and the overall program of study.

Also, further research in teacher development and training in the area of foreign language and L2 reading is necessary if the findings from the present study are to be taken advantage of in order to benefit not only instructional issues, but also student-centered concerns. These concerns focus on the learning of the foreign language and developing and attaining a certain degree of proficiency for interaction outside of the classroom. Lastly, I should underline the previous statement. The students in these classes will need to interact outside of the classroom if their education and learning is to be taken full advantage of. It is our responsibility, at the very least, to present them with as many opportunities to use the foreign language in the classroom as possible.

## FURTHER INVESTIGATION

Now that we have a better understanding of the dynamics within a literature-based FLC, it is important to further investigate other classroom environments using the guidelines and framework set by this text. What follows are suggestions that may lead to a deeper understanding of the link between cognition, discourse, and SLA. This book has set the foundation for such research to be both fruitful and interesting. It is suggested that the person interested in furthering the ideas set forth in this text begin with basic discourse analysis (one's own class for a single lesson) then move into the more complicated and involved areas of discourse analysis in other settings and environments.

- An analysis of the instruments and methodology used in determining oral proficiency for students enrolled in the foreign language courses across the curriculums of departments involved in the instruction of foreign languages is also recommended. Also, further study is needed to understand how university foreign language programs determine and measure the development of a student's oral proficiency within each course.

- An investigation into the differences or similarities between instructors that are native speakers and nonnative speakers of the L2. This study should focus not only on the type of language used in the FLC, but also on the cognitive skills of instructors and students that are apparent in the classroom talk.

- Teacher-training programs that have oral proficiency requirements (as part of the course grade or in order to enroll in the next course) within departments that are in charge of teaching foreign languages need to be better understood. This investigation should focus on the training that preservice teachers receive in order to determine the oral proficiency of their students.

- A study to investigate text-centered classroom talk of students who are native speakers as opposed to those who are not. The study may become part of an investigation of the more advanced level courses. This study would also focus on the cognitive aspects of the students' responses as well as the type of interaction between students around the texts being studied.

- The daily language use and interaction that foreign language students have outside of the FLC should be studied. This would allow us to better understand the role of the L1 environment and L2 use outside of the classroom environment for students in the building of communities of discourse in FLCs, and its effects on students' linguistic skills and communication abilities.

# CHAPTER 11

∞

# Discourse Analysis for Classroom Teachers

After all is said and read, the question may still remain: How does a regular classroom teacher go about discovering the overall patterns of talk in his or her classroom? Here is where reality steps in and makes us take a good look at how to approach classroom research for the purpose of self-reflection. Classroom teachers across the United States do not have the time to spend researching and recording hours of their own classroom communication. Although we as teachers are trained to be aware of what is "working or not" at the moment that we are teaching, it is still valuable to view our teaching from the outside in rather than from the inside out.

The reader should keep in mind that this type of classroom research is not an extremely detailed investigation for a purpose. What should be accomplished is a general holistic understanding of the patterns of communication in a L2 classroom. If instructors have time to investigate further and define their classrooms, then the resources provided within the bibliography of the present text will allow them to do so.

## AN INITIAL GUIDE

The following guide is offered as one way that instructors may approach the initial investigation of their own classrooms:

1. Make a commitment to investigating and recording more than one class period. As we are very well aware, one class period does not allow us to understand patterns of communication. For this reason, instructors need to record (audio

or video) at least one whole unit: a chapter, story, or article. This whole unit should include the introduction of what is to be read, the reading (and discussion surrounding the text), and the evaluation of the particular objectives, including a look at the methods that were used to evaluate students.

2. After recording a whole unit, sit down and take note of the number of times the students speak in comparison with you (the instructor). This is a relatively quick way of assessing "how much" of the target language is being spoken by the students. Also, notice the overall length of the students' talk in comparison to your own. It is not necessary to actually time this. If you notice that after a rather lengthy monologue on your part you allow for a one-phrase answer from a student then move into another lengthy monologue, ask yourself if there were any opportunities for expansion of the student's answer. Also ask yourself the purpose of your "minilectures."

3. After noting the amount of teacher talk versus student talk, focus on the student-to-student interaction. Do your students talk to each other about their responses to the text or do they talk to you about each other's responses? Are you the "idea filter" in the classroom? Do you have to give the idea value in order for it to be talked about? This may be the most difficult aspect of classroom interaction and talk to change. As teachers, we are viewed as the fountain of information, especially in a language classroom where we usually dominate our students linguistically. But this linguistic domination often turns into conceptual validation.

4. For at least two class periods, write down every question or statement that you make and ask yourself the purpose of these statements or questions. Do you want to define a word? Clarify a misunderstanding? Set the context? The possibilities are endless, but the effects on classroom talk are immediate.

5. After focusing on your teacher talk, then, in the same two lessons, pay attention to the student talk. What effect do the utterances that students are saying have on the overall patterns of classroom talk? Also, pay attention to the grammar for a few minutes. Are students making use of the vast array of grammatical tools available to them through your instruction? Are you providing opportunities for students to respond or initiate classroom talk?

6. Lastly, take a look at your evaluation methods for the particular unit. Does your test, quiz, or exam reflect the topics presented during classroom talk? Do you stress grammatical accuracy, but did not correct many errors when the students interacted in class? Do you ask students to define words, but do not mention the ideas or concepts that are brought about by the use of those words? Are your evaluation methods geared toward individual understanding, where a student may support a different viewpoint or do students have to try and guess what your (the instructor's) viewpoint may be in order to answer the question "right"?

By focusing on the production of language by both the student and teacher, this outline naturally leads us to a better understanding of the patterns of talk in our classrooms. Through this understanding, we are then better equipped to view and evaluate the student talk in terms of overall linguistic and cognitive development. It is also important that we help each other and put aside our academic and professional egos. We should have other teachers view our lessons and comment on what they perceive to be the patterns of classroom talk.

# CHAPTER 12

# *Grammar in Discourse*

Constructs that we believe to be salient across SLA theories based on the term "communicative" become polarized if we take into account the role of assessment in FLCs that are driven by sociocultural and sociolinguistic paradigms. As VanPatten (1998) points out, there is a void that hovers between SLA theory and classroom practice due to the various interpretations of the word and concept of "communicative." VanPatten identifies one version of "communicative" as being text driven where communicative activities are the end result of a chapter or segment. So, students first "learn" the material then they use it to communicate, even though these curriculums and texts claim to be based on a sociolinguistic theory. As exemplified by activity theory (Vygotsky 1978; Wertsch 1991), contextualized communicative tasks lead to the acquisition of a language. Viewed through contemporary foreign language texts, communicative tasks become the measure of whether a student has learned the language and not the process through which acquisition occurs.

## EMERGENT GRAMMAR

Shohamy (1994) states that a reality of FLC tests is that they evaluate knowledge of a second language testing situation and not what is entailed in the knowledge of knowing how to use and interact with a second language. True communicative classroom assessment is task based, evolving, and contextualized. The issue that guides many FLCs, and influences SLA theories as well, is the role and concept of grammar. If we take VanPatten's

(1998) other definition of "communicative," in which language acquisition is tied to communicative events where there is a negotiation of meaning that does not rely on an a priori knowledge of grammar, we begin to see a true sociolinguistic framework emerge. Communication is not the result of knowing grammar, but grammar is acquired through communication. This notion of grammar being acquired discursively through negotiating communicative tasks is what Hopper (1988) refers to as "Emergent Grammar" where grammar is seen as incomplete and in process or emergent. In this view, grammar is not a fixed set of rules one must know in order to do well on a test because the current chapter "covered" the past tense. Meaning is not grammatical. Meaning is contextual: symbols, linguistic or not, do not require a grammar to be meaningful.

The popular view of grammar in FLCs and texts is that which Hopper labels as "A Priori Grammar," which is perfectly monologic. In order to understand or learn an A Priori Grammar, we need not involve ourselves in discourse. A Priori Grammar knowledge is easily assessed in classrooms and is used to label students as being less or more communicative than others or "knowing more" Spanish, French, German, and so on.

The notion of an Emergent Grammar refocuses our attention to the validity of "communicative assessment" based on the construct of an A Priori Grammar. More clearly stated, the linguistic structure that is to be assessed as communicative takes on different criteria for being called a structure in the monologically based assessment framework that many FLCs seem to operate under; if students are tested on a priori knowledge of structures, then structures lead to communication. Schegloff (1996) assists us in viewing the validity of framing our assessment methods through Emergent Grammar by defining linguistic structure as a form that appears through action and interaction. Meaning is not the product of automatic, predisposed blueprints of language, rather, it is contingent on dialogue. So, assessment should be dialogic and discursive.

These reflections shed a new light on the "communicative tests" that many of our FLCs use daily, as well as our literature-based FLCs. As stated before, foreign language tests test language in a testing situation. Imagine a typical testing situation in a contemporary classroom. If you saw a classroom filled with students, bent over their desks, furiously filling in blanks, listening to a passage then circling the "right answer," and scribbling verb endings in the margins beside the matching vocabulary section, then you saw the typical assessment methods based on the notion of A Priori Grammar that are prevalent in foreign language curriculums. In this situation, knowledge of linguistic structures signals a "communicative student," that is, a monologic student instead of a discursive student.

This is not to say that some classrooms may indeed take the notion of task-based, discursive learning to heart. But it is quite a different story when those students who have been taught through true task-based, interactive, meaning-negotiating tasks are faced with discreet forms of assessment that define communication as the product of learning linguistic structures. FLCs, to use a metaphor, are teaching their students how to use a spoon, but are testing them with forks.

Take a look at the test banks that come with any foreign language text-book and ask if the assessment methods fit the teaching methods. If students learn a language discursively, in the true sense of "communicative," then we should develop methods of assessment that are an accurate measure and reflection of our pedagogy.

When we transfer the notion of Emergent Grammar into a literature-based FLC, the role of assessment becomes even more dialogic and hope-fully assists students in building discourse and meaning. This view of grammar is based on the emergent qualities of classroom talk, where by talking about the reading students begin to speak more and grasp a better understanding of the grammatical rules.

In terms of assessment of grammar, a literature-based FLC that evaluates grammar away from discourse and context is going against the very meaning of "communicative." The focus on explicit rules of the language passed away with the demise of the Grammar Translation Method as the most popular way of approaching L2 learning.

Naturally, the question arises: How do we treat grammar in a classroom that hopes to promote oral proficiency through the building of cognitive skills and discourse? A particularly useful approach may be "Focus on Form."

## FOCUS ON FORM

Long and Robinson provide us with a brief synopsis of focus on form: "Focus on form often consists of an occasional shift of attention to linguistic code features, by the teacher and/or one or more students, triggered by perceived problems with comprehension or production" (1998, 23).

The relevance of focus on form is seen in the statement that its use is brought about by the difficulties that students may have while communicating in the classroom. Here, grammar has taken on the role of assisting students in processing information cognitively and not in isolation or without a communicative context.

My purpose here is not to launch into a debate or investigation on focus on form. Doughty and Williams (1998) have provided a well-grounded and clear volume that addresses and delineates focus on form. Due to the very nature of our realities in FLCs, grammar instruction is an integral part of the overall framework. However, what is suggested here is that grammar instruction in a literature-based FLC need not be overt. The instructor should allow for the communicative demands of language production and negotiation of meaning to assist in cognitively focusing "grammar instruction."

Instructors may feel that a grammar lesson has to be explicit and obvious for students to benefit from the instruction. This is a good point. Students should know why a teacher is taking a few minutes to explain a certain point or construct. A FLC that focuses on classroom talk to build grammatical competence should not have to break into a fifty-minute lesson on the past tense. By the time students reach classrooms that are literature-based, grammar instruction is minimal and to the point.

# CHAPTER 13

∽

# *Discourse and Communicative Competence*

We cannot enter into the field of foreign language education, at any level, without discussing the construct of communicative competence and how it relates to discourse and my findings. Foreign language teachers have used this construct for quite some time (Savignon 1991, 1997; Hymes 1967, 1972), and rightfully so because it offers insightful perceptions into the inner workings of communication and the classroom talk. Classroom teachers should read the following information to become better acquainted with communicative competence, as well as to understand how opportunities and discourse may effect cognition and language learning.

Communicative competence can be summarized as the identification of behaviors of those considered successful at what they do, specifically, the identification of characteristics of good communicators. Interestingly, it is here where the initial importance of the listener is seen. A good communicator is not good because he or she believes him- or herself to be a good communicator. It takes a listener to interact with the speaker, to negotiate meaning, to reach intersubjectivity, and to understand what the other is trying to say. The term "behaviors" may be misleading within the current thinking of this text. We may believe that behavior is action, but in our case it is much more a reaction. If we remember the distinction made earlier between the terms "sentence" and "utterance," a sentence consists mainly of action, but an utterance consists of reaction in order to properly fulfill its meaning potential.

Communication can be thought of as getting our message across. We learn very early on, however, that success of a particular communication strategy depends on the willingness of others to understand and on the interpretation they give to our meaning. Meaning is never one-sided. Rather, it is negotiated or constructed in the interaction between the persons involved. Most of our repertoire of communication strategies develops unconsciously, through assimilation of the role models—that is, the persons we admire and would like to resemble to some extent—and the success we experience in our interactions. Classroom teachers who do not extend their understanding of communication beyond the first sentence of this paragraph are more apt to fall into a repetitive IRE pattern where students are being given information and messages that will later need repeating.

Conveyance of meaning in unfamiliar contexts requires practice in the use of the appropriate register or style of speech. If a woman wants to sound like a business executive, she has to talk the way business executives talk when they are on the job. The same register of style of speech would of course be inappropriate when talking of personal matters with a spouse or an intimate friend. Communication then is a continuous process of expression, interpretation, and negotiation, especially when the meanings we intend and the meanings others construct are not always the same. How many times have teachers (and students) said, "No, that's not what I meant. You completely misunderstood what I was trying to say." Communication through discourse relies on the opportunities to enter into extended patterns of classroom talk, especially in a FLC where the focus is on understanding a text. Classroom teachers need to become aware that the use of a text will complicate communication and discourse in their classrooms. Too often will teachers rely on a text because they believe it is easier to learn or teach from. Communication within TCT too often only reproduces the text, and, as stated before, does not produce meaning.

The following is a brief overview of communicative competence that teachers can use to remind themselves of what the goal of reaching this entails.

• Communicative competence is dynamic rather than static
• It is interpersonal
• It applies both to written as well as to spoken language
• It is context specific
• It makes use of appropriate choices of register and style

Communicative competence is relative, not absolute, and depends on the cooperation of all the participants involved. We can thus talk of degrees of communicative competence.

Members of a community will behave and interpret the behavior of others according to the knowledge of the communicative systems they have available to them. This knowledge includes but is not limited to the formal possibilities of the linguistic code. The grammatical factor is one among several factors that affect communicative competence.

Communicative competence may also be defined as the ability to function in a truly communicative setting that is in a dynamic exchange in which linguistic competence must adapt itself to the total informational input, both linguistic and paralinguistic. Success depends largely on the individual's willingness to express himself in the foreign language that he has at his command and through his knowledge of the paralinguistic features, such as intonation, facial expression, gestures, and so on. Linguistic accuracy in terms of pronunciation, grammar, and vocabulary is but one of the major constituents of this complex interaction.

The following components all have to come together during discourse in order for communicative competence to be achieved or developed. The difficulty in using such a framework with texts is that teachers may focus too much on one aspect, such as grammatical, in order to communicate their messages to the students. But by using a text, the other components are brought immediately into play when a discussion follows the reading. All of these four elements are to be nurtured and realized during classroom discourse.

- Grammatical competence: linguistic competence.
- Sociolinguistic competence: the social rules of language use/appropriateness of an utterance, which involves more than knowing what to say in a situation but also how to say it. "Don't sound too much like a native speaker in some instances." Formal and informal registers.

The following element, discourse competence, under our current framework needs to be revised in order to include the notion of utterance instead of sentence. If teachers approach discourse competence through an understanding of the sentence, then messages and communication will be seen as one-sided. In other words, as long as the speaker "says it right" then he or she has achieved a certain degree of discourse competence. However, discourse competence, renamed here as "negotiation competence," relies on the listener and writer as much as the speaker and reader.

- Negotiation competence: interpretation of a series of utterances to form a meaningful whole. Recognizing a theme or topic of a paragraph, chapter, or book, or getting the gist of a phone conversation, poem, television commercial, office memo, recipe, or legal document requires negotiation competence.

- Strategic competence: making the best use of what we do know to get our messages across. Here, communicative competence is relative. The use of strategies to compensate for an imperfect knowledge of linguistic rules also encompasses this term. Strategies used for coping with limitations in their knowledge or restrictions in the use of that knowledge. This ability to communicate with restrictions thus includes the ability to adapt one's communicative strategies to a variety of changing and often unexpected interpersonal conditions.

Communicative confidence is developed from realistic situations or opportunities. For example, problem solving involves all components of communicative competence. Strategic competence is directly related to negotiation competence.

Therefore, communicative competence is much greater than linguistic grammatical competence alone and one does not go from one to the other as one strings pearls on a necklace. Rather, an increase in one component of communicative competence interacts with the other components to produce a corresponding increase in overall communicative competence.

The ability to cope within limitations is an ever-present component of communicative competence. Whatever the relative importance of the various components at any given level of overall proficiency, it is important to keep in mind the interactive nature of their relationships. The whole of communicative competence is always something other than the simple sum of its parts.

Classroom teachers not familiar with the elements of communicative competence need to keep in mind the following points when trying to develop their students' oral proficiency. Keeping these points as essential guides will assist in structuring overall lesson plans and objectives and allow for discourse to develop as naturally as possible within the constraints of the classroom culture that was defined earlier.

- Communicative competence is a dynamic rather than a static concept that depends on the negotiation of meaning between two or more persons who share some knowledge of the language. In this sense, then, communicative competence can be said to be an interpersonal rather than an intrapersonal trait.

- Communicative competence should not be thought of as only an oral phenomenon. It applies to both written and spoken language.

- Communicative competence is context-specific, in that communication always takes place in a particular context or situation. The communicatively competent language user will know how to make appropriate choices in register and style to fit the particular situation in which communication occurs.

- It is important to bear in mind the theoretical distinction between competence and performance. Competence is what one knows. Performance is what one does. Only performance is observable, however, and it is only through performance that competence can be developed, maintained, and evaluated.

- Communicative competence is relative and depends on the cooperation of all those involved. It makes sense, then, to speak of degrees of communicative competence.

# Afterword

Readers cannot approach a text such as this one without having at least some curiosity about language and language acquisition in general. That which occupies our thoughts when we are in classrooms (as teachers or students), cafes or living rooms, builds itself into a stated or unstated philosophy of language, a philosophy that is not easily understood by the speaker or listener when communicated between friends or acquaintances.

At times, the mere mention of a philosophy of anything brings some of us to the brink of despair. Why do we need to outline a philosophy? Can they not see by the way we teach and behave what we believe? As the old saying goes "actions speak louder than words." And this may be true, but when we vocalize our beliefs to someone else, we have to contend with the ultimate listener—ourselves—and with the responsibility of understanding that is shared between the listener and the speaker. In light of this, I have been able to develop a philosophy of language that, if nothing else, should allow room for interpretation. But a philosophy is needed, not just by those in the professional and academic fields, but also by our students. These philosophies will allow them to approach life thinking and not just doing; action is good, but before action there has to be thought. If not, then it is just a mindless reflex.

As instructors then, we need to remember that the works of literature and other authentic readings that we introduce to our students are dangerously out of place. As was presented in the beginning of this text, the authors that most of us rely on in the language classrooms most likely did not have in mind the environments in which we teach when they wrote their manuscripts. I can only offer an interpretation. But I would welcome the chance to sit down and discuss with a teacher how and why a particular text that was written in another time, land, and context was meant for him or her. This would be a truly valuable insight to have.

The readings that we use in the L2 classrooms will probably have a personal appeal to us. They may remind us of a past friend, another country where we bought and read the book for the first time, or perhaps a shady spot in our grandfather's garden. This is not to say that those of us who came across the manuscripts in a classroom did not enjoy them as much or held them anymore dear to our hearts. The point here is that students deserve the opportunity to enjoy or dislike a text based on their own opinions, rather than on the interpretations of others.

We can dissect our classrooms on various levels and with dozens of theoretical and pedagogical instruments. At times, we may enjoy learning more about how we teach, how students learn, and why we do what we do. And there are other times when we will interpret the results to best suit our purposes.

Placing ourselves within the various theories or frameworks available to us will always help us feel better and focus our efforts when we come into contact with differing opinions, thus is human nature. However, the problem arises when we come into contact with different thoughts and we believe that the person expressing those thoughts wants to change our minds, to convince us, to bring us over to his or her side, when the case just might be that he or she only wants you to understand his or her position from your vantage point.

Above all, after reading this text, the reader should grasp the realization that there are no real accidents in our classrooms. We pattern our behavior, beliefs, and language according to our own personal environment. Knowing this, students are to be given the opportunities to engage us within our realms—the classroom—since we are both products and producers of each other's language, cognition, and discourse. It is when we deny the students these opportunities and resist trying to appreciate their version of understanding that language becomes recitation and reading becomes a subject.

# Appendix: Florida Taxonomy of Cognitive Behavior

## 1.00 KNOWLEDGE OF SPECIFICS

1. Reads
2. Spells
3. Identifies something by name
4. Defines meaning of "term"
5. Gives a specific fact
6. Tells about an event
7. Recognizes symbol
8. Cites rule
9. Gives chronological sequence
10. Gives steps of process, describes method
11. Cites trend
12. Names classification system or standard
13. Names what fits in a given system or standard

## 1.30 KNOWLEDGE OF UNIVERSALS AND ABSTRACTIONS

14. States generalized concept or idea
15. States a principle, law, or theory
16. Tells about organization or structure
17. Recalls name of principle, law, or theory

## 2.0 TRANSLATION

18. Restates in own words or briefer terms
19. Gives concrete example of an abstract idea
20. Verbalizes from a graphic representation
21. Translates verbalization into graphic form
22. Translates figurative statements to literal statements or vice versa
23. Translates foreign language to English or vice versa

## 3.00 INTERPRETATION

24. Gives reason (tells why)
25. Shows similarities, differences
26. Summarizes, concludes from observation of evidence
27. Shows cause and effect relationship
28. Gives analogy, simile, and metaphor
29. Performs a directed task or process

## 4.00 APPLICATION

30. Applies previous image to new situation
31. Applies principle to new situation
32. Applies abstract knowledge in particular situation
33. Identifies, selects, and carries out process

## 5.00 ANALYSIS

34. Distinguishes fact from opinion
35. Distinguishes fact from hypothesis
36. Distinguishes conclusions from statements that support it
37. Points out unstated assumption
38. Shows interaction or relation of elements
39. Points out particulars to justify conclusion
40. Checks hypothesis with given information
41. Distinguishes relevant statements from irrelevant statements
42. Detects error in thinking
43. Infers purpose, point of view, thoughts, and feelings
44. Recognizes bias or propaganda

## 6.00 SYNTHESIS (Creativity)

45. Reorganizes ideas and materials process
46. Produces unique communication, divergent idea
47. Produces a plan or a proposed set of opportunities
48. Designs an apparatus
49. Designs a structure
50. Devises scheme for classifying information
51. Formulates hypothesis, intelligent guess
52. Makes deductions from abstract propositions
53. Draws inductive generalizations from specifics
54. Evaluates something from evidence
55. Evaluates something from criteria

# Bibliography

Akyel, A., and Yalcin, E. (1990). Literature in the EFL Class: A Study of Goal-Achievement Incongruence. *ELT Journal*, 44 (3), 174–180.

Ali, S. (1994). The Reader-Response Approach: An Alternative for Teaching Literature in a Second Language. *Journal of Reading*, 37, 288–296.

Aljaafreh, A., and Lantolf, J. P. (1994). Negative Feedback As Regulation and Second Language Learning in the Zone of Proximal Development. *The Modern Language Journal*, 78, 465–483.

Allwright, D. (1984). The Importance of Interaction in Classroom Language Learning. *Applied Linguistics*, 5, 165–171.

Anderson, P. M., and Rubano, G. (1991). *Enhancing Aesthetic Reading and Response*. Urbana, IL: National Council of Teachers of English.

Anton, M. (1999). The Discourse of a Learner-Centered Classroom: Sociocultural Perspectives on Teacher-Learner Interaction in the Second Language Classroom. *The Modern Language Journal*, 83, 303–318.

Applebee, A. (1985). Studies in the Spectator Role: An Approach to Response to Literature. In *Researching Response to Literature and the Teaching of Literature: Points of Departure*, ed. C. R. Cooper, 87–102. Norwood, NJ: Ablex.

Austin, J. L. (1975). *How to Do Things with Words*. Cambridge, MA: Harvard University Press.

Bakhtin, M. M. (1986). *Speech Genres and Other Late Essays*. Austin: University of Texas Press.

———. (1984). *Problems of Dostoevsky's Poetics*. Minneapolis: University of Minneapolis Press.

———. (1981). *The Dialogic Imagination: Four Essays by M M Bakhtin*. Ed. M. Holquist. Austin: University of Texas Press.

Barnes, K. (2000). Revising a Spanish Novel Class in Light of Standards for Foreign Language Learning. *ADFL Bulletin*, 31 (2), 44–48.

Bateson, G. (1972). *Steps to an Ecology of Mind*. New York: Ballantine.

Beach, R. (1993). *A Teacher's Introduction to Reader-Response Theories*. Urbana, IL: NCTE.

Bereiter, C. (1994). Implications of Postmodernism for Science or Science As Progressive Discourse. *Educational Psychologist*, 29 (1), 3–12.

Bereiter, C., and Scarmandalia, M. (1987). *The Psychology of Written Composition*. Hillsdale, NJ: Erlbaum.

Bernhardt, E. (1995). Teaching Literature or Teaching Students? *ADFL Bulletin*, 26 (2), 5–6.

Blackbourn, B. (1986). The Transition from Language Courses to Literature: A Pragmatic Stance. *The French Review*, 60 (2), 196–202.

Bloom, B. S. (1956). *Taxonomy of Educational Objectives: Handbook I, Cognitive Domain*. New York: McKay.

Bowlby, J. (1974). *Attachment*. London: Hogarth.

Bransford, J. D. (1976). *The Role of 'Effort After Meaning' and 'Click of Comprehension' in Recall of Sentences. Final Report*. Tennessee: ERIC/ED 188208.

Breen, M. P. (1985). The Social Context for Language Learning—a Neglected Situation? *Studies in Second Language Acquisition*, 7, 135–158.

Bretz, M. L., and Persin, M. (1987). A Working Model for the Teaching of Literature at the Introductory Level. *The Modern Language Journal*, 71, 165–170.

Britton, J. (1982). *Prospect and Retrospect: Selected Essays of James Britton*. London: Heinemann.

Brooks, F. (1993). Some Problems and Caveats Communicative Discourse: Towards a Conceptualization of the Foreign Language Classroom. *Foreign Language Annals*, 26 (2), 233–242.

Brooks, F. B., et al. (1997). When Are They Going to Say "It" Right? Understanding Learner Talk during Pair-Work Activity. *Foreign Language Annals*, 30 (4), 524–540.

Brooks, F. B., and Donato, R. (1994). Vygostkian Approaches to Understanding Foreign Language Learner Discourse during Communicative Tasks. *Hispania*, 77, 262–273.

Brown, G. (1996). Language Learning, Competence and Performance. In *Performance and Competence in Second Language Acquisition*, ed. G. Brown, K. Malmkjaer, and J. Williams, 187–203. Cambridge: Cambridge University Press.

Brown, G., and Yule, G. (1983). *Discourse Analysis*. Cambridge: Cambridge University Press.

Canale, M., and Swain, M. (1980). Theoretical Bases of Communicative Approaches to Second Language Teaching and Testing. *Applied Linguisitics*, 1, 1–47.

Carrasco, R. L. (1981). Expanding Awareness of Student Performance: A Case

Study in Applied Ethnographic Monitoring in a Bilingual Classroom. In *Culture and the Bilingual Classroom: Studies in Classroom Ethnography*, ed. H. T. Trueba, G. P. Guthrie, and K. H. Au, 153–177. Rowley, MA: Newbury House.

Carter, R., and Long, M. (1990). Teaching Literature in EFL Classes: Tradition and Innovation. *ELT Journal*, 44 (3), 215–221.

Cathcart, R. (1983). Functional Analysis of Language Data. Paper presented at 17th Annual TESOL Convention, Toronto, Canada.

Cazden, C. (1986). Classroom Discourse. In *Handbook of Research on Teaching*, ed. M. C. Wittrock, 432–463. New York: Macmillan.

Celce-Murcia, M., et al. (1995). Communicative Competence: A Pedagogically Motivated Model with Content Specifications. *Issues in Applied Linguisitcs*, 6 (2), 5–35.

Chamot, A. U. (1994). A Model for Learning Strategies Instruction in the Foreign Language Classroom. *Georgetown University Round Table on Languages and Linguistics 1994*. Washington, DC: Georgetown University Press.

Chaudron, C. (1988). *Second Language Classrooms: Research on Teaching and Learning*. Cambridge: Cambridge University Press.

———. (1977). A Descriptive Model of Discourse in the Corrective Treatment of Learners' Errors. *Language Learning*, 27, 29–46.

Chou, H. V., et al. (1980). Teacher Questioning: A Verification and an Extension. *Journal of Reading Behavior*, 12, 69–72.

Coleridge, S. T. (1983). *Biographia Literaria*. Ed. J. Engell and W. J. Bate. London: Routledge and Kegan Paul.

Cooper, C. (1985). Evaluation the Results of Classroom Literary Study. In *Researching Response to Literature and the Teaching of Literature*, ed. C. Cooper. Norwood, NJ: Ablex.

Coulthard, M. C. (1977). *An Introduction to Discourse Analysis*. London: Longman.

Cupchik, G. C. (1996). Suspense and Disorientation: Two Poles of Emotionally Charged Literary Uncertainty. In *Suspense: Conceptualizations, Theoretical Analysis, and Empirical Explorations*, ed. P. Vorder, H. J. Wulff, and M. Friedrechson. Hillsdale, NJ: Erlbaum.

Curtain, H., and Pesola, C. (1994). *Languages and Children: Making the Match*. White Plains, NY: Longman.

Davidheiser, J. (1977). An Interdisciplinary Approach to the Teaching of Foreign Literature. *The Modern Language Journal*, 61, 25–31.

Davis, J. N. (1992). Reading Literature in the Foreign Language: The Comprehension/Response Connection. *The French Review*, 63 (3), 359–370.

———. (1989). The Act of Reading in the Foreign Language: Pedagogical Implications of Iser's Reader-Response Theory. *The Modern Language Journal*, 73, 420–428.

Davis, J. N., et al. (1992). Readers and Foreign Languages: A Survey of Undergraduate Attitudes toward the Study of Literature. *The Modern Language Journal*, 76, 320–331.

Delpit, L. (1998). The Politics of Teaching Literate Discourse. In *Negotiating Academic Literacies: Teaching and Learning across Languages and Cultures*, ed. V. Zamel and R. Spack, 207–218. Mahwah, NJ: LEA.

Devitt, S. (1989). Classroom Discourse: Its Nature and Potential for Language Learning. *CLCS Occasional Paper No. 21*. Trinity College, Dublin: Centre for Language and Communication Studies.

Deyes, A. F. (1974). Speech Activity in the Language Class. *ELTJ*, 28, 222–226.

Donato, R. (1994). Collective Scaffolding in Second Language Learning. In *Vygotskian Approaches to Second Language Research*, ed. J. P. Lantolf and G. Appel, 33–56. Norwood, NJ: Ablex.

Donato, R., and Adair-Hauk, B. (1992). Discourse Perspectives on Formal Instruction. *Language Awareness*, 1 (2), 73–89.

Doughty, C., and Williams, J. (1998). *Focus on Form in Second Language Acquisition*. Cambridge: Cambridge University Press.

Dressler, W. U., ed. (1978). *Current Trends in Textlinguistics*. Berlin: Walter de Gruyter.

Dunn, W. E., and Lantolf, J. P. (1998). Vygotsky's Zone of Proximal Development and Krashen's i + 1: Incommensurable Constructs; Incommensurable Theories. *Language Learning*, 48 (3), 411–442.

Eagleton, T. (1983). *Literary Theory: An Introduction*. Oxford: Basil Blackwell.

Eco, H. (2000). *Kant and the Platypus*. New York: Routledge.

Edwards, A., and Furlong, V. J. (1978). *The Language of Teaching*. London: Heinemann.

Elkind, D. (1981). *The Hurried Child: Growing up Too Fast Too Soon*. Reading, MA: Addison-Wesley.

Elliot, R. (1990). Encouraging Reader-Response to Literature in the ESL Situation. *ELT Journal*, 44 (3), 191–198.

Ellis, R. (1990). Researching Classroom Language Learning. In *Research in the Language Classroom*, ed. C. Brumfit and R. Mitchell, 54–70. London: Modern English Publications in association with the British Council.

———. (1984). *Classroom Second Language Development*. Oxford: Pergamon.

Empson, W. (1961). *Seven Types of Ambiguity*. Harmondsworth: Penguin.

Engestrom, Y. (1991). Activity Theory and Individual and Social Transformation. *Activity Theory*, 7/8, 6–17.

Fairclough, N. (1993). Critical Discourse Analysis and the Marketization of Public Discourse: The Universities. *Discourse and Society*, 4, 133–168.

Fillmore, L. W. (1982). Instructional Language As Linguistic Input: Second Language Learning in Classrooms. In *Communicating in the Classroom*, ed. L. C. Wilkinson, 283–296. New York, Academic.

Floriani, A. (1994). Negotiating What Counts: Roles and Relationships, Texts and Contexts, Content and Meaning. *Linguistics and Education* 5, 241–274.

Forman, E. A. (1995). Learning in the Context of Peer Collaboration: A Pluralistic Perspective on Goals and Expertise. *Cognition and Instruction*, 13, 549–564.

Forman, E. A., and Cazden, C. B. (1985). Exploring Vygotskian Perspectives in Education: The Cognitive Value of Peer Interaction. In *Culture, Communication and Cognition: Vygotskian Perspectives*, ed. J. V. Wertsch, 332–347. New York: Cambridge University Press.

Frake, C. O. (1997). Plying Frames Can Be Dangerous: Some Reflections on Methodology in Cognitive Anthropology. In *Mind, Culture, and Activity: Seminal Papers from the Laboratory of Human Cognition*, ed. M. Cole, Y. Engestrom, and O. Vasquez. New York: Cambridge University Press.

Freire, P. (1972). *Pedagogy of the Oppressed.* Harmondsworth, Middlesex: Penguin Books.

Frey, E. (1972). What Is Good Style? *The Modern Language Journal*, 55 (5), 310–322.

Frye, N. (1984). Literary and Linguistic Scholarship in a Post-literate World. *PMLA*, 99, 990–995.

———. (1970). *The Stubborn Structure: Essays on Criticism and Society.* London: Methuen.

Gass, S., and Varonis, E. M. (1994). Input, Interaction, and Second Language Production. *SSLA*, 16, 283–302.

Geertz, C. (1973). *The Interpretation of Cultures: Selected Essays by Clifford Geertz.* New York: Basic.

Givens, C. F. (1976). *A Descriptive Study of the Cognitive Level of Classroom Discourse of College Professors and Students.* Ph.D. diss., Claremont University.

Goodenough, W. (1971). *Culture, Language, and Society.* Reading, MA: Addison-Wesley.

Graden, E. C. (1996). How Language Teacher's Beliefs about Reading Instruction Are Mediated by Their Beliefs about Students. *Foreign Language Annals*, 29 (3), 387–395.

Grimes, J. E. (1975). *The Thread of Discourse.* The Hague: Mouton.

Halasz, L. (1989). Social Psychology, Social Cognition, and the Empirical Study of Literature. *Poetics*, 18, 29–44.

Hall, J. K. (1999). The Communication Standards in Foreign Language Education. In *Foreign Language Standards: Linking Research, Theories, and Practices*, ed. J. K. Phillips and R. M. Terry, 15–56. New York: NTC.

———. (1997). A Consideration of SLA As a Theory of Practice: A Response to Firth and Wagner. *The Modern Language Journal*, 81, 301–306.

———. (1995a). "Aw, Man, Where You Goin'?": Classroom Interaction and the Development of L2 Interactional Competence. *Issues in Applied Linguistics*, 6 (2), 37–62.

———. (1995b). (Re)creating Our World with Words: A Sociohistorical Perspective of Face-to-Face Interaction. *Applied Linguistics*, 16 (2), 206–232.

Halliday, M. A. K. (1993). Towards a Language-Based Theory of Learning. *Linguistics and Education*, 5, 93–116.

———. (1978). *Language As Social Semiotic: The Social Interpretation of Language and Meaning.* London: Arnold.

———. (1975). *Learning How to Mean*. London: Arnold.

———. (1970). Language Structure and Language Function. In *New Horizons in Linguistics*, ed. J. Lyons, 144–165. Harmondsworth: Penguin.

Hankins, O. (1972). Literary Analysis at the Intermediate Level. *The Modern Language Journal*, 55 (5), 291–295.

Harper, S. (1988). Strategies for Teaching Literature at the Undergraduate Level. *The Modern Language Journal*, 72 (4), 402–408.

Heritage, J. (1988). Current Development in Conversation Analysis. In *Conversation*, ed. D. Roger and P. Bull, 21–47. Clevedon, UK: Multilingual Matters.

Hester, R. (1972). From Reading to the Reading of Literature. *The Modern Language Journal*, 55 (5), 284–290.

Hopper, P. (1988). Emergent Grammar and the A Priori Grammar Postulate. In *Linguistics in Context: Connecting Observation and Understanding*, ed. D. Tannen. Norwood, NJ: Ablex.

Howatt, A. (1984). *A History of English Language Teaching*. Oxford: Oxford University Press.

Huebner, T., and Davis, K. A., eds. (1999). *Sociopolitical Perspectives on Language Policy and Planning in the USA*. Philadelphia, PA: Benjamins.

Hymes, D. (1981). Ethnographic Monitoring. In *Culture and the Bilingual Classroom: Studies in Classroom Ethnography*, ed. T. Trueba, G. P. Guthrie, and K. H. Au, 56–80. Rowley, MA: Newbury House.

———. (1972). On Communicative Competence. In *Sociolinguistics*, ed. J. B. Pride and J. Holmes, 269–293. Harmondsworth: Penguin.

———. (1967). *The Anthropology of Communication: Human Communication Theory*. New York: Holt, Rinehart and Winston.

Hynds, S. (1992). Challenging Questions in the Teaching of Literature. In *Literature Instruction: A Focus on Student Response*, ed. J. Langer. Urbana, IL: NCTE.

———. (1991). Questions of Difficulty in Literary Reading. In *The Idea of Difficulty in Literature*, ed. A. C. Purves. New York: State University of New York Press.

Isenberg, N. (1990). Literary Competence: The EFL Reader and the Role of the Teacher. *ELT Journal*, 44 (3), 181–190.

Iser, W. (1978). *The Act of Reading: A Theory of Aesthetic Response*. Baltimore, MD: Johns Hopkins University Press.

Johnson, K. (1995). *Understanding Communication in Second Language Classrooms*. Cambridge: Cambridge University Press.

Katz, A. (1996). Teaching Style: A Way to Understand Instruction in Language Classrooms. In *Voices from the Language Classroom: Qualitative Research in Second Language Education*, ed. K. M. Bailey and D. Nunan, 57–87. Cambridge: Cambridge University Press.

Katz, J., and Fodor, J. (1963). The Structure of Semantic Theory. *Language*, 39, 170–210.

Kaufman, W. (1996). The Inhibited Teacher. *English Journal,* 60 (3), 382-388.

Keenan, E. and Scheiffelen, B. (1976). Topic as Discourse in Notion. In *Subject and Topic*, ed. C. Li and S. Thompson. New York: Academic Press.

Kempf, F. R. (1995). The Dialectic of Education: Foreign Language, Culture, and Literature. *ADFL Bulletin*, 27 (1), 38–46.

Kerry, T. (1982). The Demands Made on Pupils Thinking in Mixed Ability Classes. In *Investigating Classroom Talk*, ed. A. D. Edwards and D. P. G. Westgate. London: Falmer.

Kintsch, W. (1988). The Role of Knowledge in Discourse Comprehension: A Construction Integration Model. *Psychological Review*, 95, 163–182.

Knutson, E. (1993*)*. Teaching Whole Texts: Literature and Foreign Language Reading Instruction. *The French Review*, 67 (1), 12–27.

Kramsch, C. (1993). *Context and Culture in Language Teaching*. Oxford: Oxford University Press.

———. (1985). Literary Texts in the Classroom: A Discourse Model. *The Modern Language Journal*, 69, 356–66.

Kumaravadivelu, B. (1999). Critical Classroom Discourse Analysis. *TESOL Quarterly*, 33 (3), 453–484.

———. (1993). Maximizing Learning Potential in the Communicative Classroom. *The Modern Language Journal*, 76 I(1), 41–49.

———. (1992). Macrostrategies for the Second/Foreign Language Teacher. *The Modern Language Journal*, 75, 12–21.

———. (1991). Language Learning Tasks: Teacher Intention and Learner Interpretation. *ELT Journal*, 47 (1), 98–10

Langer, J., ed. (1992). *Literature Instruction: A Focus on Student Response*. Urbana, IL: NCTE.

Lantolf, J. P. (2000). *Sociocultural Theory and Second Language Learning*. Oxford: Oxford University Press.

Lantolf, J. P., and Appel, G. (1994). *Vygotskian Approaches to Second Language Research*. Norwood, NJ: Ablex.

Lave, J. (1977). Tailor-Made Experiments and Evaluating the Intellectual Consequences of Apprenticeship Training. *Quarterly Newsletter of the Laboratory of Comparative Human Cognition*, 1, 1–3.

Lave, J., and Wegener, E. (1991). *Situated Learning: Legitimate Peripheral Participation*. New York: Cambridge University Press.

Lazar, G. (1993). *Literature and Language Teaching: A Guide for Teachers and Trainers*. Cambridge: Cambridge University Press.

———. (1990). Using Novels in the Language-Learning Classroom. *ELT Journal*, 44 (3), 204–214.

Lazarus, R. S. (1984). On the Primacy of Cognition. *American Psychologist*, 39, 124–139.

Leal, L. (1999). The Spanish Short Story and Its Potential for the Secondary and College Classroom. *1971 ACTFL Meeting Manuscript*, Chicago.

Learner, G. H. (1994). Responsive List Construction: A Conversational Resource for Accomplishing Multifaceted Social Action. *Journal of Language and Social Psychology*, 13, 20–33.

Lemke, J. L. (1990a). The Language of Classroom Science. In *Locating Learning across the Curriculum*, ed. C. Emihovich, 216–239. Norwood, NJ: Ablex.

———. (1990b). *Talking Science: Language, Learning, and Values.* Norwood, NJ: Ablex.

———. (1985). *Using Language in the Classroom.* London: Oxford University Press.

Leontiev, A. A. (1981). *Psychology and the Language Learning Process.* Oxford: Permagon.

Liaw, M. (2001). Exploring Literary Responses in an EFL Classroom. *The Foreign Language Annals* 34 (1), 35–45.

Lightbown, P. (1990). Process-Product Research on Second Language Learning in Classrooms. In *The Development of Second Language Proficiency*, ed. B. Harley et al., 82–92. Cambridge: Cambridge University Press.

Lincoln, Y., and Guba, E. (1985). *Naturalistic Inquiry.* Beverly Hills, CA: Sage.

Littlewood, W. (1981). *Communicative Language Teaching: An Introduction.* Cambridge: Cambridge University Press.

———. (1980). Form and Meaning in Language-Teaching Methodology. *Language Journal*, 64 (4), 441–445.

Long, M. H. (1997). Construct Validity in SLA Research: A Response to Firth and Wagner. *The Modern Language Journal*, 81, 318–323.

———. (1996). The Role of Linguistic Environment in Second Language Acquisition. In *Handbook of Second Language Acquisition*, ed. W. C. Ritchie and T. K. Bhatia, 414–468. New York: Academic.

———. (1985a). Input and Second Language Acquisition Theory. In *Input in Second Language Acquisition*, ed. S. M. Gass and C. Madden, 377–393. Rowley, MA: Newbury House.

———. (1985b). A Role for Instruction in Second Language Acquisition: Task-Based Language Training. In *Modelling and Assessing Second Language Acquisition*, ed. K. Hyltsenstam and M. Peinemann, 77–99. Clevedon, UK: Multilingual Matters.

———. (1983). Native Speaker/Non-Native Speaker Conversation and the Negotiation of Comprehensible Input. *Applied Linguistics*, 4, 126–141.

———. (1981). Input, Interaction, and Second Language Acquisition. In *Native Language and Foreign Language Acquisition*, ed. H. Winitz, 379, 259–278. New York: Annals of the New York Academy of Sciences.

Long, M. H., and Crookes, G. (1986). Intervention Points in Second Language Classroom Processes. *RELC*, 21–25 April.

Long, M. H., and Porter, P. A. (1985). Group Work, Interlanguage Talk, and Second Language Acquisition. *TESOL Quarterly*, 19 (2), 207–227.

Long, M. H., and Robinson, P. (1998). Focus on Form: Theory Research and Practice. In *Focus on Form in Classroom Second Language Acquisition*, ed. C. Doughty and J. Williams. Cambridge: Cambridge University Press.

Long, M. H., and Sato, C. (1983). Classroom Foreigner Talk Discourse: Forms and Functions of Teachers' Questions. In *Classroom Oriented Research in Second Language Acquisition*, ed. H. W. Seliger and M. H. Long. Rowley, MA: Newbury House.

Lotman, Y. M. (1988). Text within a Text. *Soviet Psychology*, 26 (3), 32–51.

Loureda Lamas, O. (1999). Acerca del Objeto y los Objetivos de la Ensenanza del Area de la Lengua y la Literatura en la Ensenanza Secundaria Obligatoria. *RILCE*, 15 (2), 427–438.

Luria, A. R. (1981). *Language and Cognition*. Ed. J. V. Wertsch. New York: Wiley.

Lyons, J. (1977). *Semantics*. Cambridge: Cambridge University Press.

Mackey, A. (1999). Input, Interaction, and Second Language Development: An Emperical Study of Question Formation in ESL. *Studies in Second Language Acquisition*, 21, 557–587.

Markee, N. (2000). *Conversation Analysis*. Hillsdale, NJ: Erlbaum.

McCarthy, J. A. (1998). W(h)ither Literature? Reaping the Fruit of Language Study before It's Too Late. *ADFL Bulletin*, 29 (2), 10–36.

Meade, R. (1980). On Teaching Literature in Today's World. *Hispania*, 63, 36–39.

Miall, D. S., and Kuiken, D. (1994). Foregrounding, Defamiliarization, Affect: Response to a Short Story. *Poetics*, 22, 389–407.

Moskowitz, G. (1976). The Classroom Interaction of Outstanding Foreign Language Teachers. *The Foreign Language Annals*, 9 (2), 135–157.

Mukarovsky, J. (1977). *The Word and Verbal Art*. Ed. and trans. J. Burbank and P. Steiner. New Haven, CT: Yale University Press.

Murray, D. (1982). *Learning by Teaching*. Portsmouth, NH: Heinemann.

Myunskins, J. A. (1983). Teaching Second Language Literatures: Past Present and Future. *The Modern Language Journal*, 67, 413–423.

Myunskins, J. A., and Cassini, J. (1991). Literature in the Foreign Language: A Comparative Study. In *International Perspectives on Foreign Language Teaching*, ed. G. Ervin, 138–159. Lincolnwood, IL: NTC.

Nunan, D. (1989). *Designing Tasks for the Communicative Classroom*. Cambridge: Cambridge University Press.

———. (1987). Communicative Language Teaching: Making It Work. *ELT Journal*, 41 (2), 136–145.

Osborn, T. A. (2000). *Critical Reflection and the Foreign Language Classroom*. Westport, CT: Bergin and Garvey.

———. (1998). Providing Access: Foreign Language Learners and Genre Theory. *The Foreign Language Annals*, 31 (1), 40–47.

Peck, J. (1985). Advanced Literary Study As Cultural Study: A Redefinition of the Discipline. *The Modern Language Journal*, 85, 49–53.

Pennycook, A. (1998). Borrowing Other's Words: Text, Ownership, Memory, and Plagiarism. In *Negotiating Academic Literacies: Teaching and Learning across Languages and Cultures*, ed. V. Zamel and R. Spack, 265–292. Mahwah, NJ: LEA.

Pertosky, A. (1992). To Teach Literature? In *Literature Instruction: A Focus on Student Response*, ed. J. A. Langer. Urbana, IL: NCTE.

Pica, T. (1987). Second-Language Acquisition, Social Interaction, and the Classroom. *Applied Linguistics*, 8 (1), 3–21.

Pica, T., and Long, M. (1986). The Linguistic and Conversational Performance of Experienced and Inexperienced Teachers. In *Talking to Learn*, ed. R. Day, 85–98. Rowley, MA: Newbury House.

Platt, E., and Brooks, F. B. (1994). The "Acquisition-Rich Environment" Revisited. *The Modern Language Journal*, 78, 497–511.

Purves, A. C. (1985). That Sunny Dome: Those Caves of Ice. In *Researching Response to Literature and the Teaching of Literature: Points of Departure*, ed. C. Cooper. Norwood, NJ: Ablex.

Ricouer, P. (1976). *Interpretation Theory: Discourse and the Surplus of Meaning*. Fort Worth: Texas University Press.

Rogoff, B. (1990). *Apprenticeship in Thinking: Cognitive Development in Social Context*. New York: Oxford University Press.

Rogoff, B., and Wertsch, J. V., Eds. (1984). *Children's Learning in the Zone of Proximal Development*. San Francisco: Jossey-Bass.

Rommetveit, R. (1979a). Deep Structure of Sentence versus Message Structure: Some Critical Remarks on Current Paradigms, and Suggestions for an Alternative Approach. In *Studies of Language, Thought, and Verbal Communication*, ed. R. Rommetveit and R. M. Blakar. London: Academic.

———. (1979b). On the Architecture of Intersubjectivity. In *Studies of Language, Thought, and Verbal Communication*, ed. R. Rommetveit and R. M. Blakar, 93–108. London: Academic.

Rosenblatt, L. M. (1938). *Literature As Exploration*. New York: MLP.

Sacks, H. (1972). On the Analizability of Stories by Children. In *Directions in Sociolinguistics*, ed. J. Gumperz and D. Hymes, 325–345. New York: Holt, Rinehart and Winston.

Sacks, H., Schlegoff, E., and Jefferson, G. (1974). A Simplest Systematics for the Organization of Turn-Taking in Conversation. *Language*, 50, 696–735.

Santoni, G. V. (1971). Methods of Teaching Literature. Annual Meeting of ACTFL, 25–28 November.

Sapir, E. (1921). *Language: An Introduction to the Study of Speech*. New York: Harcourt Brace.

De Saussure, F. (1983). *Course in General Linguistics*. Chicago: Open Court.

Savignon, S. (1997). *Communicative Competence: Theory and Classroom Practice*. 2nd ed. New York: McGraw-Hill

———. (1991). Communicative Language Teaching: State of the Art. *TESOL Quarterly*, 25, 261–277.

Schegloff, E. (1996). Turn Organization: One Intersection of Grammar and Interaction. In *Interaction and Grammar*, ed. E. Ochs et al. Cambridge: Cambridge University Press.

Schiffrin, D. (1994). *Approaches to Discourse*. Massachusetts: Blackwell Publishers.

———. (1990). Conversational Analysis. *Annual Review of Applied Linguistics*, 11, 3–19.

———. (1987). *Discourse Markers*. Cambridge: Cambridge University Press.

———. (1986). Turn-Initial Variation: Structure and Function in Conversation. In *Diversity and Diachrony*, ed. D. Sankoff, 367–380. Philadelphia, PA: Benjamins.

Searle, J. R. (1969). *Speech Acts*. Cambridge, MA: Harvard University Press.

Selinker, L. (1972). Interlanguage. *IRAL*, 10 (3), 31–51.

Shlosvsky, V. (1965). Art As Technique. In *Russian Formalist Criticism: Four Essays*, ed. L. T. Lemon and M. J. Reis. Lincoln: University of Nebraska Press.

Shohamy, E. (1994). The Validity of Direct versus Semi-direct Oral Tests. *Language Testing*, 11, 99–124.

Sinclair, J. and Coulthard, M. (1975). *Towards and Analysis of Discourse*. London: Oxford University Press.

Skutnabb-Kangas, T. (2000). *Linguistic Genocide in Education—or Worldwide Diversity and Human Rights*. Mahwah, NJ: Erlbaum.

Slobin, D. (1991). Learning to Think for Speaking: Native Language, Cognition, and Rhetorical Style. *Pragmatics*, 1, 7–26.

Smagorinsky, P. (1993). The Social Environment of the Classroom: A Vygotskian Perspective on Small Group Processes. *Communication and Education*, 42 (2), 159–171.

Smithson, J. L. (1995). Describing the Enacted Curriculum: Development and Dissemination of Opportunity to Learn Indicators in Science Education. Paper Commissioned by the SCASS Science Project, Washington, DC.

De Sousa, R. (1987). *The Rationality of Emotion*. Cambridge: Massachusetts Institute of Technology Press.

Spada, N. (1987). Relationships between Instructional Differences and Learner Outcomes: A Process-Product Study of Communicative Language Teaching. *Applied Linguistics*, 8 (2), 137–161.

Steiner, F. (1972). Teaching Literature in the Secondary Schools. *The Modern Language Journal*, 55 (5), 278–283.

———. (1970). Teaching Literature by Performance Objectives. *Foreign Language Annals*, 3, 579–591.

Stone, R. (1990). The Motivation to Study Literature. *Babel*, 25 (3), 18–21.

Swaffar, J. (1998). Major Changes: The Standards Project and the New Foreign Language Curriculum. *ADFL Bulletin*, 30 (1), 34–37.

Swain, M. (1985). Communicative Competence: Some Roles of Comprehensible Input and Comprehensible Output and Its Development. In *Input in Second Language Acquisition*, ed. S. Gass and C. Madden, 235–253. Rowley, MA: Newbury House.

Taylor, D. S. (1985). Teaching Reading for Comprehension in the Context of English As a Second or Foreign Language. *British Journal of Language Teaching*, 23 (3), 163–168.

Tharp, R. G., and Gallimore, R. (1988). *Rousing Minds to Life: Teaching, Learning, and Schooling in Social Context.* Cambridge: Cambridge University Press.

Thomas, J. J. (1998). Is There Still a Place for Linguistics in the Foreign Language and Literature Curriculum? *ADFL Bulletin,* 30 (1), 25–29.

Tobin, K. (1997). Dialectical Constraints to the Discourse Practices of a High School Physics Community. *Journal of Research in Science Teaching,* 34, 491–507.

Todorov, T. (1984). *Mikhail Bakhtin: The Dialogical Principal.* Minneapolis: University of Minnesota Press.

Trueba, H. T. (1989). *Raising Silent Voices: Educating the Linguistic Minority for the 21st Century.* New York: Newbury House.

Tudge, J. (1990). Vygotsky, the Zone of Proximal Development, and Peer Collaboration: Implications for Classroom Practice. In *Vygotsky and Education: Instructional Implications and Applications of Sociohistorical Psychology,* ed. L. C. Moll, 155–172. Cambridge: Cambridge University Press.

Tudor, I. (1993). Teacher Roles in Learner-Centered Classrooms. *ELT Journal,* 47 (1), 22–31.

Vande Berg, C. K. (1993). Managing Learner Anxiety in Literature Courses. *The French Review,* 67 (1), 27–37.

Van Dijk, T. (1997). *Discourse As Structure and Process: Discourse Studies.* London: Sage.

———. (1979). Cognitive Processing of Literary Discourse. *Poetics Today,* 1, 143–159.

VanPatten, B. (1998). Perceptions of and Perspectives on the Term "Communicative." *Hispania,* 81, 925–932.

———. (1993). Grammar Teaching for the Acquisition-Rich Classroom. *Foreign Language Annals,* 26 (4), 435–450.

Van Vliet, L. W. (1992). *Approaches to Literature through Genre.* Phoenix, AZ: Oryx.

Volosinov, V. N. (1973). *Marxism and the Philosophy of Language.* New York: Seminar.

Vygotsky, L. S. (1981). *The Genesis of Higher Mental Functions.* Cambridge, MA: Harvard University Press.

———. (1978). *Mind in Society.* Cambridge, MA: Harvard University Press.

———. (1962). *Thought and Language.* Cambridge: Massachusetts Institute of Technology Press.

Walz, J. (1993). Context and Contextualized Language Practice in Foreign Language Teaching. *The Modern Language Journal,* 73 (2), 160–168.

Webb, J. N. (1970). The Florida Taxonomy of Cognitive Behavior. In *Mirrors for Behavior, an Anthology of Classroom Observation Instruments,* ed. A. Simon et al. Philadelphia: Research for Better Schools.

Wells, G. (1999). *Dialogic Inquiry: Toward Sociocultural Practice and Theory of Education.* Cambridge: Cambridge University Press.

————. (1993). Reevaluating the IRF Sequence: A Proposal for the Articulation of Theories of Activity and Discourse for the Analysis of Teaching and Learning in the Classroom. *Linguistics and Education*, 5, 1–37.

Wertsch, J. V. (1998). *Mind As Action*. Oxford: Oxford University Press.

————. (1991). *Voices of the Mind: A Sociocultural Approach to Mediated Action*. Cambridge, MA: Harvard University Press.

————, ed. (1986). *The Concept of Activity in Soviet Psychology*. Armonk, NY: Sharpe.

Whorf, B. L. (1956). *Language, Thought, and Reality: Selected Writings of Benjamin Lee Whorf*. Ed. J. B. Carroll. Cambridge: Massachusetts Institute of Technology Press.

Wood, D. (1992). Teaching Talk. In *Thinking Voices: The Work of the National Oracy Project*, ed. K. Norman. London: Hodder and Straughton.

Woods, C. A. (1986). On the Seashore of the Worlds: Play and Potential in English. *English Education*, 18 (4), 197–208.

# Index

**About the Author**

MIGUEL MANTERO is Assistant Professor of Foreign Language and English as a Second Language at The University of Alabama.